PATHWAYS

Reading, Writing, and Critical Thinking

4B

Laurie Blass   Mari Vargo   Keith S. Folse, Series Consultant

NATIONAL GEOGRAPHIC LEARNING

HEINLE
CENGAGE Learning

Australia • Brazil • Japan • Korea • Mexico • Singapore • Spain • United Kingdom • United States

Pathways Split Text 4B
Reading, Writing, and Critical Thinking
Laurie Blass and Mari Vargo
Keith S. Folse, Series Consultant

Publisher: Andrew Robinson

Executive Editor: Sean Bermingham

Associate Development Editor: Ridhima Thakral

Contributing Editor: Karen Davy

Director of Global Marketing: Ian Martin

International Marketing Manager:
  Caitlin Thomas

Director of Content and Media Production:
  Michael Burggren

Senior Content Project Manager: Daisy Sosa

Manufacturing Buyer: Marybeth Hennebury

Cover Design: Page 2, LLC

Cover Image: Alaska Stock Images/
  National Geographic Creative

Interior Design: Page 2, LLC

Composition: Page 2, LLC

ISBN 13: 978-1-285-45710-9
ISBN 10: 1-285-45710-2

Cengage Learning Asia Pte Ltd
151 Lorong Chuan #02-08
New Tech Park (Lobby H)
Singapore 556741

National Geographic Learning
20 Channel Center Street
Boston, MA 02210
USA

Cengage Learning is a leading provider of customized learning solutions with office locations around the globe, including Singapore, the United Kingdom, Australia, Mexico, Brazil, and Japan. Locate your local office at:
ngl.cengage.com

Cengage Learning products are represented in Canada by Nelson Education, Ltd.

Visit National Geographic Learning online at **ngl.cengage.com**

Visit our website at **www.cengageasia.com**

Printed in Singapore
1 2 3 4 5 6 7 8 16 15 14 13

Contents

	Scope and Sequence	vi
	Explore a Unit	viii
6	Language and Culture	119
7	Resources and Development	141
8	Living Longer	165
9	Memorable Experiences	189
10	Imagining the Future	211
	Video Scripts	238
	Independent Student Handbook	243
	Vocabulary and Skills Index	251

▲ Deforestation creates a mountain of logs in Alberta, Canada. **page 2**

▲ A memorial in Gloucester, Massachusetts honors the memory of sailors lost at sea. **page 198**

▲ Denmark is the world's leading producer of wind-generated energy. **page 76**

THEY THAT GO
DOWN TO THE SEA
IN SHIPS
• 1623 ― 1923 •

In the seas east of Yucatan peninsula, Mexico, a school of sardines uses swarm techniques to defend against a sailfish attack. **page 102**

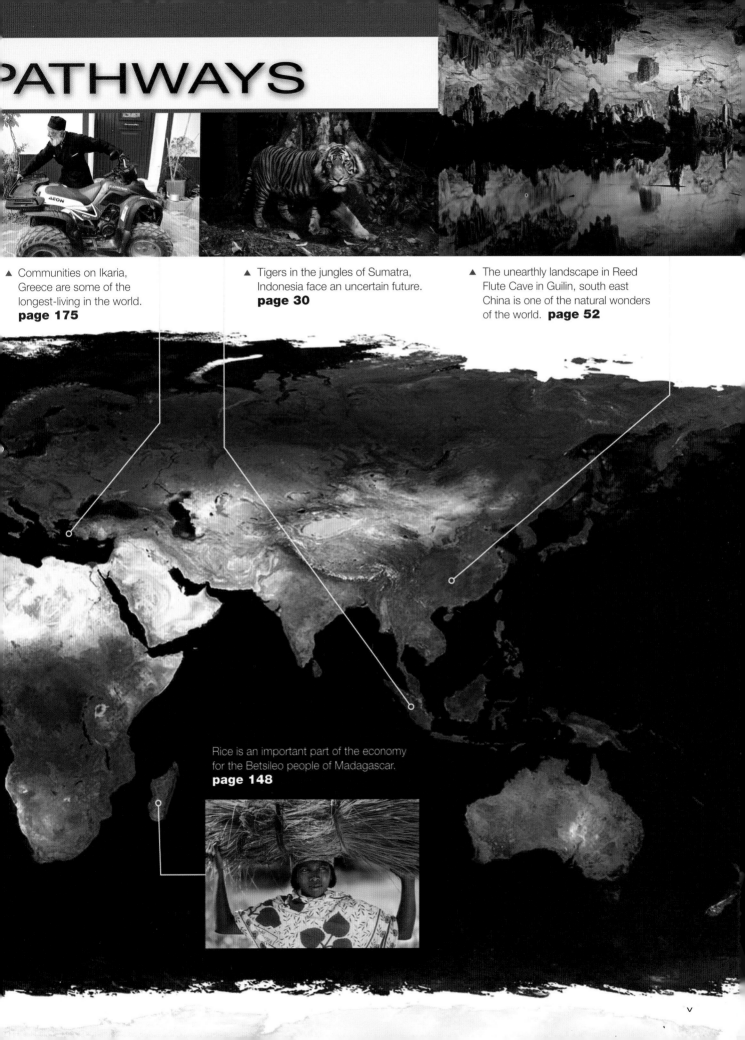

PATHWAYS

▲ Communities on Ikaria, Greece are some of the longest-living in the world. **page 175**

▲ Tigers in the jungles of Sumatra, Indonesia face an uncertain future. **page 30**

▲ The unearthly landscape in Reed Flute Cave in Guilin, south east China is one of the natural wonders of the world. **page 52**

Rice is an important part of the economy for the Betsileo people of Madagascar. **page 148**

Scope and Sequence

Unit	Academic Pathways	Vocabulary
6 **Language and Culture** *Page 119* Academic Track: Interdisciplinary	**Lesson A:** Inferring an author's attitude Understanding verbal phrases **Lesson B:** Writing introductions and conclusions Writing a personal opinion essay	Understanding meaning from context Using vocabulary to complete definitions Applying vocabulary in a personalized context **Word Link:** *ir-; con-; crypt*
7 **Resources and Development** *Page 141* Academic Track: History/Economics	**Lesson A:** Identifying a writer's point of view Understanding cohesion (II) **Lesson B:** Researching and note-taking Writing an expository essay	Understanding meaning from context Using vocabulary to complete definitions Applying vocabulary in a personalized context **Word Partners:** *tension*
8 **Living Longer** *Page 165* Academic Track: Health and Medicine	**Lesson A:** Predicting a conclusion Asking questions as you read **Lesson B:** Planning a research paper Writing an argumentative research paper	Understanding meaning from context Using vocabulary to complete definitions Applying vocabulary in a personalized context **Word Link:** *struct; uni-*
9 **Memorable Experiences** *Page 189* Academic Track: Interdisciplinary	**Lesson A:** Making inferences Analyzing a personal narrative **Lesson B:** Using sensory details Writing an extended personal narrative	Understanding meaning from context Using vocabulary to complete definitions Applying vocabulary in a personalized context **Word Usage:** *ensure/insure* **Word Partners:** *assumption*
10 **Imagining the Future** *Page 211* Academic Track: Interdisciplinary	**Lesson A:** Reading literature critically Identifying literary elements **Lesson B:** Writing critically about literature Writing an analysis of fiction excerpts	Understanding meaning from context Using vocabulary to complete definitions Applying vocabulary in a personalized context **Word Link:** *liter* **Word Partners:** *flee/fled*

Reading	Writing	Viewing	Critical Thinking
The Secret Language By Daisy Zamora (autobiographical essay) Identifying main ideas and key details **Skill Focus:** Understanding verbal phrases	**Goal:** Writing a personal opinion essay about language learning **Language:** Adding information with verbal phrases **Skill:** Writing introductions and conclusions	**Video:** *Kenyans in New York* Viewing to confirm predictions Viewing for general understanding and specific information Relating video content to reading texts	Analyzing types of language Personalizing an author's experience Synthesizing to make a comparison Analyzing an introduction and a conclusion Analyzing a model essay **CT Focus:** Inferring an author's attitude
The Shape of Africa By Jared Diamond (expository/persuasive essay) Identifying chronology Identifying main ideas and key details **Skill Focus:** Understanding cohesion (II)	**Goal:** Writing an expository essay about a country or region's development **Language:** Referring to sources **Skill:** Researching and note-taking	**Video:** *The Encroaching Desert* Activating prior knowledge Viewing for general understanding and specific information Relating video content to reading texts	Evaluating a writer's text organization Synthesizing to make an interpretation Evaluating and applying research information Analyzing a model essay **CT Focus:** Identifying a writer's point of view
Beyond 100 By Stephen S. Hall (explanatory scientific article) Identifying main ideas and key details identifying supporting examples Understanding infographics **Skill Focus:** Asking questions as you read	**Goal:** Writing an argumentative research paper about longevity **Language:** Explaining the significance of evidence **Skill:** Planning a research paper	**Video:** *Secrets of a Long Life* Viewing to confirm predictions Viewing for general understanding and specific information Relating video content to reading texts	Making inferences from an infographic Synthesizing to make inferences Evaluating research topics and evidence Analyzing a model essay **CT Focus:** Predicting a conclusion
Welcome Stranger By Sebastian Junger (personal narrative) Identifying purpose and structure Identifying key details **Skill Focus:** Analyzing a personal narrative	**Goal:** Writing an extended personal narrative about a past experience **Language:** Reviewing past forms **Skill:** Using sensory details	**Video:** *Frontline Diary* Viewing to confirm predictions Viewing for general understanding and specific information Relating video content to reading texts	Personalizing an author's experience Synthesizing to make hypotheses Analyzing an author's sensory details Applying information Analyzing a model essay **CT Focus:** Making inferences about a text
My Mars and extracts from ***The Martian Chronicles*** By Ray Bradbury (autobiographical essay/fiction extracts) Identifying main ideas and key details **Skill Focus:** Identifying literary elements	**Goal:** Writing an analysis of fiction excerpts **Language:** Using a variety of sentence types **Skill:** Writing critically about literature	**Video:** *Mission: Mars* Viewing to confirm predictions Viewing for general understanding and specific information Relating video content to reading texts	Interpreting figurative language Inferring motivation and purpose Synthesizing to make hypotheses Evaluating analysis topics and evidence Analyzing a model essay **CT Focus:** Reading literature critically

EXPLORE A UNIT

Each unit has two lessons.

Lesson A develops academic reading skills and vocabulary by focusing on an important contemporary theme. The language and content in these sections provide the stimulus for a guided writing task (Lesson B). A video section acts as a content bridge between Lessons A and B.

The **unit theme** focuses on an academic content area relevant to students' lives, such as Health Science, Business and Technology, and Environmental Science.

Academic Pathways highlight the main academic skills of each lesson.

Exploring the Theme provides a visual introduction to the unit. Learners are encouraged to think critically and share ideas about the unit topic. Authentic charts, maps, and graphics from National Geographic help learners comprehend key ideas and develop visual literacy.

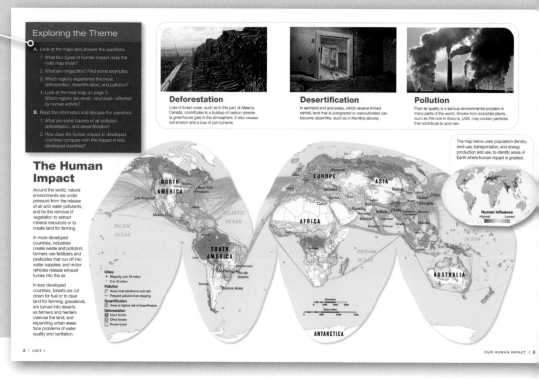

In **Preparing to Read**, learners are introduced to key vocabulary items from the reading passage. Guided pre-reading tasks and strategy tips encourage learners to think critically about what they are going to read.

The **Reading** passage is an authentic text related to the unit theme. Reading texts include magazine articles, book extracts, and passage from literature. Each reading passage is recorded on the audio program.

B | Building Vocabulary. Complete the sentences with the words from the box. Use a dictionary to help you.

compound	concept	criteria	incorporate	register	shifting

1. As a result of global warming, some bird species are moving to new places. For example, the North American warbler is _____ its habitat 65 miles to the north.

2. One of the _____ for naming a new animals species is that the name must be easy to remember.

3. Researchers have recently discovered that a combination of chemicals in a common weed killer, a _____ called POE-15, can have a serious effect on human health.

4. If you _____ an invention with the patent office, your idea will go into an official record, and it will be protected so that it cannot be copied.

5. A basic scientific _____ is cause and effect—the idea that an event is caused by or affected by another event.

6. To _____ something means to include it within something that already exists.

▲ An endangered golden-cheeked warbler

LESSON A   READING

THE HUMAN AGE

by Elizabeth Kolbert

Human beings have altered the planet so much in just the past century or two that we now have a new name for a new epoch: the Anthropocene.

Guided comprehension tasks and reading strategy instruction enable learners to improve their academic literacy and critical thinking skills.

UNDERSTANDING THE READING

A | Identifying Main Ideas. Write answers to the questions.

1. What is the purpose of Kolbert's article? Complete the main idea.

   Kolbert's purpose is to present the idea of a new _____ and to show how our human impact will be noted in the future.

2. What does "Anthropocene" mean? Explain it in your own words.

   _____

   _____

3. The reading passage has three main parts. Where could you place each of these section heads? Write paragraph letters: A, H, and N.

Section Head	Before Paragraph . . .
How We Are Changing the Planet	_____
Tracing the Origins of the Anthropocene	_____
A New Perspective on Earth's History	_____

4. What four main areas does Kolbert examine for signs of human impact?

   cities, _____

B | Identifying Key Details. Write answers to the questions.

1. When was the idea of a new era first proposed? What was it called?

   _____

2. What do cities basically consist of, according to Kolbert? Why might cities not be visible in the future?

   _____

   _____

3. How do fertilizers and industrial farming affect the environment?

   _____

Critical Thinking tasks require learners to analyze, synthesize, and critically evaluate the ideas and information in the reading.

C | Critical Thinking: Evaluating. Use your answers to exercise **B** to complete the chart summarizing the human impact. Then discuss this question in a small group: Of the four kinds of human impact, which do you think will leave the most obvious record in the future? Why?

	The Human Effect	Will It Leave a Trace? Why, or Why Not?
Cities	by building _____ structures	No—structures built on land; _____ may make them disappear
Farming	by using fertilizers	_____—but only from the _____ record of the shift from a variety of plants to a few types
Forests	by _____	Maybe—sedimentation and _____ may be noticed
Atmosphere	by _____ the atmosphere	Most likely—shifts in habitat range will leave traces in _____; _____ of the world's oceans and corals will cause _____

D | Understanding Infographics. Look at the infographic on page 10 and answer the questions. Then discuss your answers with a partner.

1. What is the main purpose of the infographic? Circle the best answer.
   a. to show the importance of changes in human technology since 1900
   b. to show how different factors have contributed to our human impact
   c. to show how population growth has risen faster than affluence

2. Look at the "I=PAT" formula. What does it mean? Explain it in your own words.

   _____

   _____

3. Describe how the following factors have increased since 1900.

   population: _____

   GDP (affluence): _____

   technology: _____

CT Focus: Analyzing arguments

An argument usually presents a debatable issue and includes evidence that supports the issue. When you read a passage that presents an argument, first identify the issue—the writer's argument. Then analyze the writer's evidence. Is it fully developed? Is it accurate? Is it detailed? Is it current? How do you know?

E | Critical Thinking: Analyzing Evidence. In the reading on pages 6–12, what evidence does the writer present in support of either side of the main issue? Take notes in the chart. Then discuss answers to the questions below with a partner.

Issue: Our impact on the planet is so great that we are now living in a new epoch.

Arguments For	Arguments Against

1. Are the arguments on both sides equally balanced, or is there more evidence for one side than the other?

2. Are we at the start of a new epoch? Should we name the current period "Anthropocene"? Why, or why not?

F | Identifying Meaning from Context. Find and underline the following words and expressions in the reading passage. Use context to guess their meanings. Then match the sentence parts.

1. _____ Paragraph A: If a word is **coined by** someone,
2. _____ Paragraph C: If an idea **struck a chord,**
3. _____ Paragraph D: If a concept is **picked up,**
4. _____ Paragraph J: If something is **life-throttling,**
5. _____ Paragraph M: If a consequence is **discernible,**
6. _____ Paragraph O: If you **stave off** an event,
7. _____ Paragraph P: When something **drags on,**

a. it moves slowly.
b. you can detect it.
c. other people thought it sounded logical.
d. you prevent it from happening.
e. people decide to adopt it.
f. it was invented by that person.
g. it causes things to die.

Reading Skill: Understanding Cohesion

Cohesion is the way that ideas are linked in a text. Writers use certain techniques (sometimes called "cohesive devices") to refer to ideas mentioned elsewhere in the passage. Some of these techniques include pronouns (one[s], another, the other), demonstratives (this, that, these, those), and synonyms.

Look at these examples from "The Human Age."

In 2002, when Crutzen wrote up the Anthropocene idea in the journal Nature, the concept was immediately picked up by researchers working in a wide range of disciplines.

The writer uses a synonym, *the concept*, to refer to *the idea* in the first part of the sentence.

Wilson calculates that human biomass is already a hundred times larger than that of any other large animal species that has ever walked the Earth.

In this example, the writer uses *that* to refer to *biomass*.

Note: The referent—the word or idea that is referred to—is not always close to the cohesive device. It may be in a different part of the sentence, or in a different sentence or section of the text.

A | Analyzing. Circle the word or idea that each underlined word in these extracts refers to.

1. Paragraph D: "Global Analysis of River Systems: From Earth System Controls to Anthropocene Syndromes" ran the title of one 2003 paper. "Soils and Sediments in the Anthropocene" was the headline of <u>another</u>, published in 2004.

   a. title   b. paper   c. river system

2. Paragraph H: But it turns out most cities are not good candidates for long-term preservation for the simple reason that they're built on land, and on land the forces of erosion tend to win out over <u>those</u> of sedimentation.

   a. forces   b. cities   c. candidates

B | Analyzing. Find the following excerpts in "The Human Age." Write the words or ideas that each underlined words or phrases refer to.

1. Paragraph E: At first, most of the scientists using <u>the new geologic term</u> were not geologists. _____

2. Paragraph F: The boundaries between epochs are defined by changes preserved in sedimentary rocks—the emergence of one type of commonly fossilized organism, say, or the disappearance of <u>another</u>. _____

3. Paragraph L: Probably the most significant change, from a geologic perspective, is <u>one</u> that's invisible to us—the change in the composition of the atmosphere. _____

4. Paragraph M: The most recent <u>one</u>, which is believed to have been caused by the impact of an asteroid, took place 65 million years ago, at the end of the Cretaceous period. _____

Viewing tasks related to an authentic National Geographic video serve as a content bridge between Lessons A and B. (Video scripts are on pages 235–242.)

VIEWING   **Man-Made Earthquakes**

Before Viewing

A | Using a Dictionary. Here are some words you will hear in the video. Match each one with the correct definition. Use a dictionary to help you.

excavation	extract	induced	perturb	stress (v.)

1. _____ disturb greatly
2. _____ the act of digging in the earth
3. _____ put pressure on
4. _____ caused; triggered
5. _____ take out; remove

B | Thinking Ahead. Discuss these questions with a partner: What are some examples of materials that are mined? What are some possible positive and negative effects of mining?

_____

_____

_____

While Viewing

B | Read the questions (1–5). Think about the answers as you view the video.

1. Where did the earthquake described in the video occur?
2. What were the effects of this earthquake?
3. What was a possible cause of the earthquake?
4. What are "pre-existing conditions"? How do earthquakes affect them?
5. What percentage of earthquakes around the world may be caused by mining?

After Viewing

A | Discuss the answers to the questions in exercise **B** in "While Viewing" with a partner.

B | Critical Thinking: Synthesizing. How does mining contribute to the human impact on the planet?

▼ Gold miners at Serra Pelada Mine, Brazil

The **Goal of Lesson B** is for learners to relate their own views and experience to the theme of the unit by completing a guided writing assignment.

Integrated **grammar practice and writing skill development** provides scaffolding for the writing assignment.

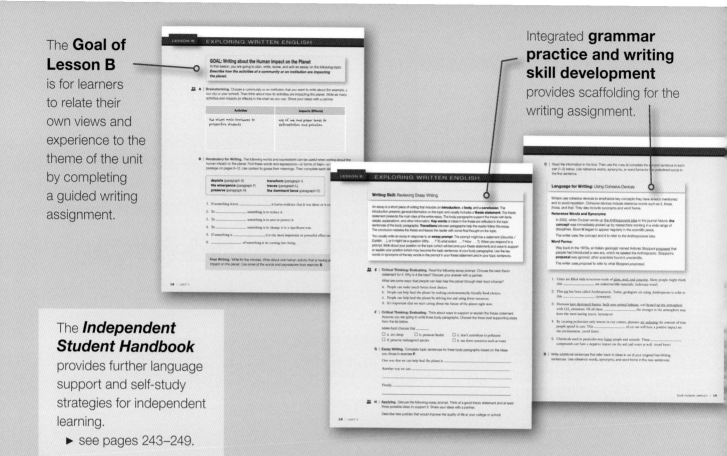

The **Independent Student Handbook** provides further language support and self-study strategies for independent learning.
▶ see pages 243–249.

Resources for *Pathways* Level 4

Video DVD with authentic National Geographic clips relating to each of the ten units.

Teacher's Guide
including teacher's notes, expansion activities, rubrics for evaluating written assignments, and answer keys for activities in the Student Book.

Audio CDs with audio recordings of the Student Book reading passages.

A **guided process approach** develops learners' confidence in planning, drafting, revising, and editing their written work.

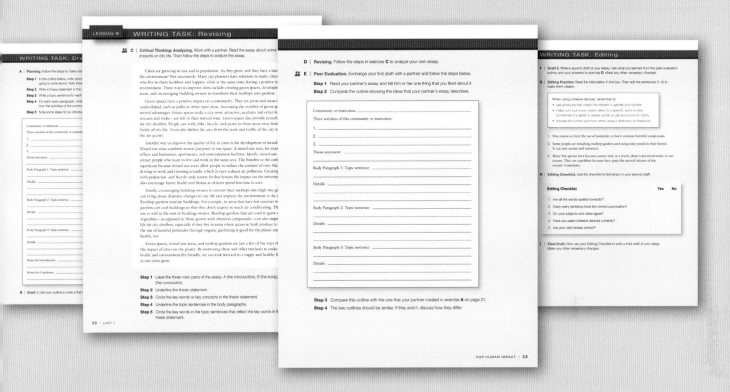

Assessment CD-ROM with ExamView®

containing a bank of ready-made questions for quick and effective assessment.

Classroom Presentation Tool CD-ROM featuring

audio and video clips, and interactive activities from the Student Book. These can be used with an interactive whiteboard or computer projector.

Online Workbook, powered by MyELT,

with both teacher-led and self-study options. This contains the 10 National Geographic video clips, supported by interactive, automatically graded activities that practice the skills learned in the Student Books.

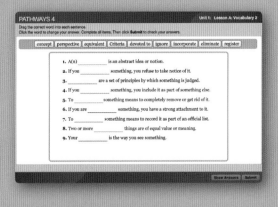

Text

124-128 Adapted from "The Secret Language" by Daisy Zamora, reprinted with permission of the National Geographic Society from the book "How I Learned English." Edited by Tom Miller. Copyright ©2007 Tom Miller **146-152** Adapted from "The Shape of Africa," by Jared Diamond: NGM September 2005 **171-177** Adapted from "On Beyond 100," by Peter S. Hall: NGM May 2013 **194-199** Adapted from "Welcome Stranger," by Sebastian Junger: National Geographic Adventure magazine May 2006. Copyright © 2006 by Sebastian Junger. Reprinted by permission of the Stuart Krichevsky Literary Agency, Inc. **216-218** Adapted from "My Mars," by Ray Bradbury: NGM Special Issue "Space," October 2008 **194-199** Excerpts from "The Martian Chronicles," by Ray Bradbury. Reprinted by permission of Don Congdon Associates, Inc. Copyright © 1950, renewed 1977 by Ray Bradbury

NGM = National Geographic Magazine

Photos, Illustrations and Maps

IFC: Courtesy of Don Usner; Courtesy of Daisy Zamora; Evan Agostini/Getty Images; Alberto E. Rodriguez/WireImage/Getty Images; Linda Makarov/NGC; Courtesy of Stephen S. Hall; AP Photo/Peter Dejong; Jim Spellman/WireImage/Getty Images; Courtesy of Peter Miller on behalf of NGC; Ron Galella Collection/Getty Images **i:** Chris Gray/NGC **iii:** Paul Chesley/NGC; Steve Winter/NGC; Jef Meul/Minden Pictures; Michael Melford/NGC; David Alan Harvey/NGC; Justin Guariglia/NGC; Chris Johns/NGC; Fritz Hoffmann/NGC; Joel Sartore/NGC; NASA Images **iv:** James L. Stanfield/NGC; Raul Touzon/NGC; Andrew Henderson/NGC; Mauricio Handler/NGC **iv-v:** NASA Goddard Space Flight Center Image by Reto Stöckli (land surface, shallow water, clouds) **v:** Gianluca Colla/NGC; Steve Winter/NGC; Raymond Gehman/NGC; Chris Johns/NGC **vi:** Tyrone Turner/NGC; Stephen Alvarez/NGC; Gianluca Colla/NGC; Frans Lanting/NGC; Twentieth Century-Fox Film Corporation/The Kobal Collectiom/Picture Desk **119:** Justin Guariglia/NGC **120-121:** Frans Lanting/NGC **124:** Medford Taylor/NGC **126:** Tyrone Turner/NGC **127:** John G Ross/Photo Researchers/Getty Images **133:** Mike Theiss/NGC **141:** Lynn Johnson/NGC **142-143:** National Geographic Maps **144:** Andrew Aitchison/Alamy **146-147:** Art by Kees Veenenbos based on satellite image by Earth Observatory, NASA Goddard Space Flight Center **148:** Frans Lanting/NGC **149:** Chris Johns/NGC **150:** Frans Lanting/NGC **151:** Stephen Alvarez/NGC **156:** Chris Johns/NGC **165:** Gianluca Colla/NGC **166-167:** National Geographic Maps **171, 173:** Fritz Hoffmann/NGC **174:** NGM ART/National Geographic **175:** Gianluca Colla/NGC **176:** Oliver Uberti/NGC **177:** Fritz Hoffmann/NGC **181:** Gianluca Colla/NGC **189:** Aaron Huey/NGC **190-191:** Frans Lanting/NGC **194:** Joel Sartore/NGC **196:** James P. Blair/NGC **197:** Thomas J. Abercrombie/NGC **198:** Raul Touzon/NGC **203:** Reza/NGC **211:** Anthony Fiala/NGC **212-213:** Courtesy of Michael Whelan **214:** Twentieth Century-Fox Film Corporation/The Kobal Collection/Picture Desk **216:** NASA/NGC **218:** NASA/NGC **219:** NASA Images **220:** NASA/NGC **222:** Ludek Pesek/NGC **227:** NASA/NGC **234:** Charles Fries Prods/The Kobal Collection **243, 255:** Joel Sartore/NGC **256:** James L. Stanfield/NGC

IFC = Inside Front Cover   NGC = National Geographic Creative

Language and Culture

ACADEMIC PATHWAYS

Lesson A: Inferring an author's attitude
Understanding verbal phrases

Lesson B: Writing introductions and conclusions
Writing a personal opinion essay

Think and Discuss

1. What are some benefits of being able to use a second or foreign language?

2. What do you think is the most difficult thing about learning a new language?

▲ Young students in Shanghai, China, read a lesson from their textbook. Globally, there are estimated to be more than one billion students learning English.

▲ Schoolchildren pose for a photo near Hustain Nuruu, Mongolia. Although Russian is still the most commonly spoken foreign language among older people in Mongolia, increasing numbers of young Mongolians are studying English.

Exploring the Theme

Read the information and discuss the questions.

1. What are two reasons that parents in many countries send their children to English–language schools at an early age?

2. At what age do you think people should begin learning a second language? Why?

3. Do you think language learning becomes easier or more difficult as you get older? In what ways?

According to many linguists, children are able to learn new languages more easily than adults. Research shows that we may be born with a natural, or innate, ability to learn language. Changes that occur in the brain as we age may make language learning progressively more difficult. This doesn't mean that older people cannot learn a language. In fact, adults have some advantages over children in a classroom setting. For example, they can already read, they have the discipline to study, and they are usually motivated to learn.

However, since children appear to have an innate language-learning ability, there is a trend worldwide for countries to introduce foreign language learning at an earlier age. In Europe, most children begin studying English between the ages of six and nine. In Korea, where English-language kindergartens are growing in popularity, children often begin learning English between the ages of three and five. And in China, some parents send children as young as two years old to private language schools to learn English. Only time will tell whether studying English at such an early age is an effective strategy.

A | Building Vocabulary. Read the following paragraph about reading fiction. Use the context to guess the meanings of the words and phrases in **blue**. Then write the correct word or phrase to complete each definition (1–7).

Word Link

ir = *not*: **ir**rational, **ir**regular, **ir**replaceable, **ir**resistible, **ir**reparable

For many people, certain fiction books have a special meaning. A story that a person read when they were young, for example, can make them **nostalgic** for their childhoods. But why should people read fiction? Those who enjoy reading may not have ever considered that question. They simply find reading fiction **irresistible**—when they see a new novel, they want to pick it up. If you love fiction, you might feel it's impossible to feel any other way about books. **On the contrary**, some people are not interested in fiction at all. They find reading fiction **monotonous** and boring, or they feel the formal language of literature is **unintelligible**. Many people prefer reading nonfiction or the news because the language is more **straightforward** and easier to understand. However, some researchers believe they have found **definitive** proof that reading fiction is actually beneficial for the human brain. A research team at the University of Toronto led by professor Maja Djikic, for example, found that people who read literary fiction become more open-minded and creative in their thinking, and are also better able to deal with uncertainty.

1. You use "_____" when you have just said or implied that something is not true and you are going to say that the opposite is true.

2. Something that is _____ is very boring because it has a regular, repeated pattern that never changes.

3. If you describe something as "_____," you approve of it because it is easy to do or understand.

4. Something that is _____ provides a firm conclusion that cannot be questioned.

5. When you feel _____, you think affectionately about the past.

6. If you describe something as "_____," you mean that it is so good or attractive that you cannot stop yourself from liking it or wanting it.

7. If something is _____, it is impossible to understand because it is not written or pronounced clearly or because its meaning is confused or complicated.

B | Building Vocabulary. Complete the definitions (1–5) with words from the box. Use a dictionary to help you.

> contemporaries   cryptic   excluded   integral   perpetual

Word Link

con = *together, with*: **con**done, **con**sensus, **con**temporary, **con**vene

Word Link

crypt = *hidden*: **crypt**, **crypt**ic, en**crypt**

1. A(n) _____ remark or message contains a hidden meaning or is difficult to understand.

2. A(n) _____ act, situation, or state is one that seems never to end or change.

3. If someone is _____ from a place or an activity, that person is prevented from entering it or joining it.

4. Someone's _____ are people who are or were alive at the same time as that person is or was.

5. Something that is a(n) _____ part of something is an essential part of that thing.

C | Using Vocabulary. Answer the questions. Share your ideas with a partner.

1. Are there any types of food or drink that you find **irresistible**?

2. Do any books, songs, or foods make you **nostalgic** for the past? Explain.

3. For what reasons might someone be **excluded** from an activity or a place?

D | Brainstorming. Discuss your answers to this question in small groups: What are some different ways to learn new words or phrases in a foreign language?

studying song lyrics _____

_____

_____

E | Predicting. Read the first and last paragraphs of the reading passage on pages 124–127. What kind of reading is this? Circle your answer and check your prediction as you read the rest of the passage.

     a. a scientific article

     b. a personal essay

     c. a short fiction story

The Secret Language

by Daisy Zamora

▲ A replica Mississippi steamboat
heads out from New Orleans.

> Language can be a barrier—
> but also a window through
> which we experience new
> visions of the world.

track **2-01**

A THE FIRST WORDS I HEARD IN ENGLISH were from my grandmother Ilse Gamez, who I remember as a magical presence in my childhood. Everything about her seemed legendary to me. Among the stories she used to tell, my favorites were about her life in New Orleans, where she and her family arrived from Europe and where she spent her childhood until she was 14, when they set sail again, bound for Nicaragua, fulfilling her parents' wish to return **definitively** to their country of origin. Her stories of New Orleans were filled with references and names in English (frequently also in French), and those mysterious words, so different from the ones I heard in everyday speech, produced in me an **irresistible** fascination. They sounded like strange music, an exotic melody coming from faraway fantastic places where life had an agitation,[1] a rhythm, an acceleration[2] unknown and unheard-of in the peaceful world I shared with my parents, sisters, and brothers. We were all part of an enormous family that included grandparents, great-aunts, great-uncles, uncles, aunts, and first cousins, as well as a second and third level of blood relatives, followed immediately by all the other people in the category of relatives included in the family universe and its state of **perpetual** expansion.

B The English I heard from my grandmother Ilse had nothing to do with the English I was taught in kindergarten through songs teaching us to count from one to ten, or the language that appeared in the English textbooks we studied in the second and third grade of primary school: "See Dick. See Jane. See Spot. See Puff. See Spot run. See Puff jump." For me, that English lacked charm, instead sounding like the noise of my shoes crunching in the gravel of the schoolyard during recess. But that other English, the one my grandmother and her sisters spoke, possessed multiple and varied registers[3] that always amazed me. Sometimes it sounded like the trill of a bird, light and crystalline, and at other times flowed in dense, thick amber[4] like honey. It would

rise in high notes with the lonely, **nostalgic** sound of a flute, or swirl in a whirlpool like the frenzied crowds I imagined rushing around the streets of a big metropolis . . .

C Before long, my ears began to discern another way of speaking the language. It was not the **cryptic** and fantastic English full of attractions and mystery that I loved to listen to, nor the tiresome, repetitious one that sounded like a cart struggling over cobbled streets. No, this other English expressed things in a different way that was not enigmatic[5] and seductive, nor dumb and **monotonous**, but dramatic and direct: whatever the characters said, happened simultaneously. That is to say, a word was an act; words and action occurred at the same time. An activity was named at the very moment it took place. For example, a character that was evidently crying, would say: "I'm crying." Another one, obviously hiding something, would declare: "I'll hide this!"

D It was the English I started to learn from cartoons on television, where the characters expressed thoughts, emotions, and feelings in a **straightforward** way: "Out! Help! Stop it! Don't go away! I'll be back! Let's go!" I learned phrases and words that communicated necessity in a fast, precise manner. The language of cartoons also introduced me to metaphors. The first time I heard characters in a downpour shouting their heads off with the phrase "The sky is falling, the sky is falling!" I believed it was the proper way to say in English, "It's a downpour," or "It's raining very hard."

---

[1] If someone is in a state of **agitation**, he or she is very worried or upset.
[2] An **acceleration** is an increase in speed.
[3] A **register** is a variety of language used in a specific situation.
[4] **Amber** is a hard yellowish substance that is often used as jewelry.
[5] Someone or something that is **enigmatic** is mysterious and difficult to understand.

◀ Mardi Gras
celebrations
on Bourbon
Street in
the French
Quarter of
New Orleans

E   I had no choice but to learn yet another kind of English from cowboy movies, because my cousins constantly used it in their games. Also, in a mechanical way, I learned by heart the English names for all the plays in baseball, the most popular sport in Nicaragua.

F   Gradually, the English that was so dull to me in the first grades of school expanded and deepened, with readings transforming it into a beautiful language that kept growing inside, becoming more and more a part of my consciousness, invading my thoughts and appearing in my dreams. Understanding the language and speaking it in a natural way became **integral** to my being, my way of appreciating literature, especially poetry, and enjoying the lyrics of my favorite songs, which I was able to repeat perfectly.

G   Literature classes were my favorite. To act as a character in any of Shakespeare's plays, or to read an O. Henry short story out loud to my classmates, or a chapter of Robert Louis Stevenson's *Treasure Island*, or a sonnet[6] by Elizabeth Barrett Browning,

brightened my day. At the school library, I discovered, among other authors, Walt Whitman, Emily Dickinson, and Edna St. Vincent Millay, then Carl Sandburg and William Carlos Williams. Further along, I encountered William Blake, the sisters Brontë, Jane Austen, and Ernest Hemingway. Years later, while at university, I read the Americans William Faulkner, Ezra Pound, and Gertrude Stein, and the Irish authors William Butler Yeats and James Joyce.

H   Along with my intense reading, I also became a music lover and put together a rather substantial collection of Frank Sinatra and Beatles records—my favorites, although my interests included many other groups and singers in English. From that deep relationship with the language, I wound up with what I considered a broad and complex knowledge of English, the sounds of which captivated me in the first years of life.

I   But my true encounter with living English (that is, the one spoken in everyday life) happened in the United States, where I went to spend my school vacations in

---

[6] A **sonnet** is a special type of poem with 14 lines and regular rhymes.

Middletown, Connecticut. My first impression of the country was completely idyllic. My aunt and uncle's house, where I would stay for three months, was a beautiful and comfortable three-story building, an old New England manor with a gorgeous garden out back, an orchard, a stable with horses, and a pond full of trout. A dense woods of birch and a variety of pine and spruce trees, crisscrossed by narrow paths dotted with wildflowers, went around the edge of that peaceful pond in a landscape that seemed like it was lifted from a fairy tale. Those vacations are part of the happy memories of my life because I also had the unforgettable experience of going to New York City for the first time and visiting the 1964 World's Fair. However, what is most deeply imprinted in my memory of that first visit to the U.S. is the shock I received from the language I had believed I understood and spoke correctly.

Almost immediately, I realized that my English, that is, the English through which I expressed myself, sounded strange to everybody. My cousins, not to mention their friends, listened to me with surprise or mocking looks. In turn, their English was almost **unintelligible** to me because they spoke, of course, in teenage slang. When one of my cousins couldn't stand it anymore, she told me that I was a weirdo, that I spoke like a philosopher, some sort of Socrates or something, and asked me to make an effort to try to talk like normal people so I could make some friends. She didn't have a clue about the extreme anguish I was going through trying to understand what was being said around me, trying to decipher everything I misunderstood, assuming one thing

for another. Desolate, I thought about the abundant literature I had read up to then, and the songs I had worked so hard to memorize. It was all worthless for learning to speak practical English that would help me establish bonds with boys and girls my own age. **On the contrary**, the vocabulary I learned from books, especially from the poetry that taught me to love the language, had no place in the everyday speech of my **contemporaries**.

To be accepted by everybody, I started paying extreme attention to how I expressed myself and to the words I chose. I anxiously searched for ways to adapt my way of speaking, imitating what I heard from others, so I wouldn't be **excluded** from their conversations or activities. I understood that if I didn't do that, I would be left on the fringes of the main current, the mainstream where all U.S. teenagers lived, with space only for themselves. The barrier was not easy to cross, and when I couldn't do it, my consolation was to take refuge in the library of the house, where I read, during that first vacation, an English translation of Fyodor Dostoevsky's *Crime and Punishment*.

I was 14 years old when I went to the States for the first time—the same age as my grandmother Ilse when she watched New Orleans fade into the distance from the deck of a steamship—and ever since then I've understood what it means to live in direct contact with a language through the people who speak it, through their culture, and through their vision of the world.

▼ The 1964 World's Fair in New York City

Writers of the World

During her first vacation overseas, Daisy Zamora describes seeking refuge in her family library, where the literary treasures included an English translation of Dostoevsky's *Crime and Punishment*. Today, as shown below, Dostoevsky remains one of the world's most translated authors. Several other of Zamora's favorite writers appear in this Top 50: Shakespeare, Stevenson, and Hemingway have been translated from English into many other languages.

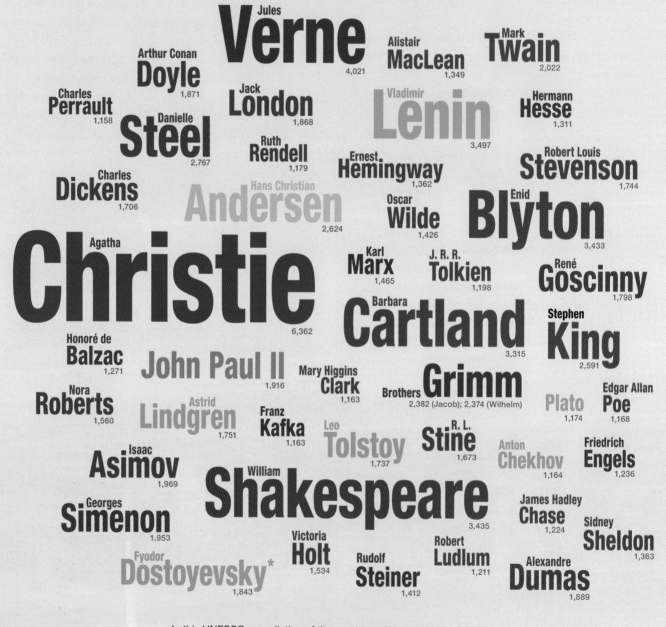

Jules **Verne**
4,021

Alistair **MacLean**
1,349

Mark **Twain**
2,022

Arthur Conan **Doyle**
1,871

Charles **Perrault**
1,158

Jack **London**
1,868

Vladimir **Lenin**
3,497

Hermann **Hesse**
1,311

Danielle **Steel**
2,767

Ruth **Rendell**
1,179

Ernest **Hemingway**
1,362

Robert Louis **Stevenson**
1,744

Charles **Dickens**
1,706

Hans Christian **Andersen**
2,624

Oscar **Wilde**
1,426

Enid **Blyton**
3,433

Agatha **Christie**
6,362

Karl **Marx**
1,465

J. R. R. **Tolkien**
1,198

René **Goscinny**
1,798

Honoré de **Balzac**
1,271

John Paul II
1,916

Barbara **Cartland**
3,315

Stephen **King**
2,591

Nora **Roberts**
1,560

Astrid **Lindgren**
1,751

Mary Higgins **Clark**
1,163

Brothers **Grimm**
2,382 (Jacob); 2,374 (Wilhelm)

Plato
1,174

Edgar Allan **Poe**
1,168

Franz **Kafka**
1,163

Leo **Tolstoy**
1,737

R. L. **Stine**
1,673

Anton **Chekhov**
1,164

Friedrich **Engels**
1,236

Isaac **Asimov**
1,969

William **Shakespeare**
3,435

James Hadley **Chase**
1,224

Georges **Simenon**
1,953

Victoria **Holt**
1,534

Rudolf **Steiner**
1,412

Robert **Ludlum**
1,211

Sidney **Sheldon**
1,363

Fyodor **Dostoyevsky***
1,843

Alexandre **Dumas**
1,889

In this UNESCO compilation of the most translated authors, size of last name corresponds to the number of translations (listed below name). Color indicates language of original publication.

■ English ■ German ■ French ■ Russian ▨ Danish
▨ Ancient Greek ■ Italian/Latin/Polish ■ Swedish

Dostoyevsky is an alternate spelling of *Dostoevsky*

A | Identifying Main Ideas. In the reading on pages 124–127, Zamora describes the different ways she experienced English. Write the correct paragraph letter(s) next to each method (1–6).

A/B	B	C/D	F/G	H	I/J

1. _____ by reading literature

2. _____ by encountering native speakers in the U.S. (her cousins)

3. _____ as a child, from her family (grandmother)

4. _____ from TV and movies

5. _____ from her school

6. _____ by listening to music

B | Identifying Key Details. Match each type of English (1–5) with Zamora's description of it.

1. her grandmother's English   _____ a. impossible to understand

2. the English in primary school   _____ b. mysterious words

3. the English in cartoons   _____ c. a fast, precise manner

4. the English of literature   _____ d. lacked charm

5. the English of her cousins   _____ e. brightened her day

CT Focus: Inferring an Author's Attitude

An author's use of language can help us understand his or her **attitude** toward, or feelings about, a subject. For example, in personal essays or narratives, writers often use figurative or sensory language to convey their feelings now or in the past. When Zamora describes her grandmother as "a magical presence in my childhood," we can infer that she had—and probably still has—a warm and loving feeling toward her grandmother, even though she doesn't state that explicitly.

C | Critical Thinking: Inferring an Author's Attitude. Write answers to the questions (1–4) and discuss your answers with a partner.

1. How does Zamora describe her grandmother's English? What does she compare it to? What can we tell about her feelings about this language?

_____

_____

_____

2. What does Zamora tell us about the English she learned at school? What two sounds does she compare it to? What can we infer about her feelings about this type of language?

_____

_____

_____

3. What adjectives and phrases does Zamora use to describe her childhood vacation home in Connecticut? What does she compare the landscape to? What can we infer about her feelings toward that place today?

_____

_____

_____

4. How does Zamora describe her experience of speaking with teenagers in the United States? Who does Zamora's cousin compare her to? What can we infer about how Zamora felt at that time?

_____

_____

_____

D | **Identifying Meaning from Context.** Find and underline the following phrases in the reading passage on pages 124–127. Use context to help you identify the meaning of each phrase (1–8). Then match each phrase with its definition.

1. _____ Paragraph A: **unheard-of**

2. _____ Paragraph B: **had nothing to do with**

3. _____ Paragraph D: **shouting their heads off**

4. _____ Paragraph H: **wound up with**

5. _____ Paragraph J: **not to mention**

6. _____ Paragraph J: **didn't have a clue**

7. _____ Paragraph J: **had no place in**

8. _____ Paragraph K: **on the fringes of the main current**

a. didn't know anything about
b. yelling loudly
c. left out or excluded from the most popular group
d. was completely unrelated to
e. eventually had
f. nonexistent
g. plus; in addition
h. didn't belong in

E | Critical Thinking: Analyzing Types of Language. Find one example of teenage language from the reading. Add four more examples of English words or phrases that teenagers say. Then discuss how the English found in literature and textbooks is different from teenage English. Complete the chart and share your ideas in a small group.

Teenage Language	How Is the Language in Literature Different?	How Is the Language in Textbooks Different?

F | Personalizing. Write an answer to the question below. Then share your answer in a small group.

How does being a language learner help you understand Zamora's essay?

_____

_____

_____

_____

_____

_____

Reading Skill: Understanding Verbal Phrases

Verbals are forms of verbs that are used as other parts of speech. The three kinds of verbals are present participles (*going, speaking*), past participles (*scared, surprised*), and infinitives (*to speak, to try*). A verbal phrase is a phrase that begins with a verbal. Writers often use verbal phrases to vary their sentence patterns and to combine short sentences. Verbal phrases are sometimes separated from the rest of the sentence with commas.

***Speaking slowly**, she gave me directions to the train station.* =
She spoke slowly. She gave me directions to the train station.

*I had a whole conversation in Spanish, **surprised I was able to communicate at all**.* =
I had a whole conversation in Spanish. I was surprised I was able to communicate at all.

***To learn Japanese quickly**, I didn't allow myself to speak English for a month.* =
I wanted to learn Japanese quickly. I didn't allow myself to speak English for a month.

A | **Analyzing.** Underline the verbal phrases in these sentences from the reading. Some sentences have more than one verbal phrase. Then write answers to the questions. Share your answers with a partner.

Example: For me, that English lacked charm, <u>instead sounding like the noise of my shoes crunching in the gravel of the schoolyard during recess.</u>

What does the verbal phrase describe? _____ the type of English _____

1. The first time I heard characters in a downpour shouting their heads off with the phrase "The sky is falling, the sky is falling!"

   Who does the verbal phrase describe? _____

2. Gradually, the English that was so dull to me in the first grades of school expanded and deepened with readings transforming it into a beautiful language that kept growing inside, becoming more and more a part of my consciousness, invading my thoughts and appearing in my dreams.

   What activity does the first verbal phrase describe? _____

   What do the second and third verbal phrases describe? _____

3. She didn't have a clue about the extreme anguish I was going through trying to understand what was being said around me, trying to decipher everything I misunderstood, assuming one thing for another.

   Who do the three verbal phrases describe? _____

4. To be accepted by everybody, I started paying extreme attention to how I expressed myself and to the words I chose.

   What does the verbal phrase do: ask a question, give a reason, or describe a thing? _____

Kenyans in

▲ A tour bus drives through Times Square in New York City.

Before Viewing

A | Using a Dictionary. Here are some words and phrases you will hear in the video. Match each word or phrase with the correct definition. Use your dictionary to help you.

grab (something)	graze like cows	stretch (our) legs

1. _____ (*informal*) eat snacks throughout the day in place of full meals
2. _____ walk around after sitting for a long period of time
3. _____ get; pick up quickly

B | Thinking Ahead. Imagine you are from a small rural community and you are arriving in a large city for the first time. What things might you find surprising? Make a list with a partner.

While Viewing

A | Watch the video about two Kenyans visiting New York City. As you watch, check your answers to exercise **B**, above. Circle the topics that are mentioned in the video.

B | Read questions 1–4. Think about the answers as you view the video.

1. What are some things that surprised the two visitors from Kenya?
2. What new words and phrases did the Kenyans pick up from their guide?
3. How does one Kenyan compare an ATM with a goat?
4. Do you think these men would find your hometown more or less surprising than New York City?

After Viewing

A | Discuss your answers to the questions 1–4 above with a partner.

B | Critical Thinking: Synthesizing. Consider the challenges that the Kenyans and Daisy Zamora had when they came to the United States for the first time. In what ways were their experiences similar and different? Who do you think had more difficulty adapting? Why?

GOAL: Writing a Personal Opinion Essay

In this lesson, you are going to plan, write, revise, and edit an essay on the following topic:

Write an opinion essay about the best way to learn a language.

Language for Writing: Adding Information with Verbal Phrases

You can add information to your sentences and vary your sentence patterns by using verbal phrases.

A present or past participial verbal phrase consists of a verbal with an adverb or an adverbial phrase (a phrase that modifies a verb). You can use a present or past participial verbal phrase like an adjective. It can modify a noun, a pronoun, or a whole clause.

pronoun   present participial verbal phrase

He looked totally confused, **staring at the teacher with his mouth open**.

past participial verbal phrase   pronoun

***Totally confused**, he* stared at the teacher with his mouth open.

An infinitive verbal phrase consists of an infinitive verb with an object or other modifier. Infinitive verbal phrases often express reasons or purposes. They can also modify a whole clause.

infinitive verbal phrase   clause

***To improve his grade**, he hired a tutor*.

infinitive verbal phrase   clause   infinitive verbal phrase

To improve his grade**, he hired a tutor **to help him study.

(Do not use a comma if the infinitive phrase comes at the end of the sentence.)

A | Circle the correct verbal phrase to complete each sentence (1–4).

1. **To teach** / **Teaching** / **Taught** their children to read, parents have to make it a point to read aloud books that are interesting to their children.

2. **To excite** / **Exciting** / **Excited** by the events in a story, children have a purpose for listening as someone reads to them—they need to find out what happens next.

3. **To look** / **Looking** / **Looked** for meaning as they listen, children begin to learn that reading has value.

4. **To increase / Increasing / Increased** vocabulary, children need to hear and read words they don't know.

B | **Analyzing.** Find the features (a–f) in the following introduction and conclusion. Underline them and write the correct letter next to each feature. Share your answers with a partner.

a. thesis statement
b. general information about the topic
c. surprising statement, interesting question, quotation, or story
d. restatement of thesis
e. explanation of how points fit together
f. final thought

Writing Skill: Writing Introductions and Conclusions

The first paragraph of an essay—the introductory paragraph—includes the thesis statement and general information about the essay topic. To grab the reader's attention, you can start with a surprising statement, an interesting question, a quotation, or a brief story.

The last, or concluding, paragraph of an essay should give the reader a sense of completeness. The conclusion usually includes a restatement of the thesis, an explanation of how the points made in the paper fit together, and a final thought about the topic. This final thought can take the form of a provocative question or a prediction about the future.

Introduction:

Nelson Mandela once said, "If you talk to a man in a language he understands, that goes to his head. If you talk to him in his own language, that goes to his heart." In other words, you can only truly communicate with another person if you speak that person's language. While the ability to communicate with someone who speaks a different language is a great benefit of language learning, I believe that studying a second language can improve our lives in other ways.

Conclusion:

Learning anything new can increase our knowledge and experience of life. However, language learning benefits us in several ways, even if we never plan to use a second language. Studying a second language can improve our reading skills and listening skills in our own language. Having better reading and listening skills can make us better students. Studies show that language learning can also improve our memories and our problem-solving skills. These abilities can help us in school, at work, and in life in general. Moreover, scientists have recently discovered that studying a second language can actually change the brain's shape. These changes can help us become better thinkers. Considering all these benefits of learning a new language, why would anyone choose not to study a second language?

C | Brainstorming. Refer back to your ideas for exercise **D** on page 123. Choose the three best methods for learning English. Complete the chart below with reasons that each method is effective. Include some examples from your own experience. Share your ideas with a partner.

Methods			
Reasons and Examples			

D | Vocabulary for Writing. You can use phrases such as "I think," "I believe," and "In my opinion" to introduce your opinion. However, varying your phrases can add interest to your writing. Some of the phrases below can introduce personal opinions, and some can introduce general opinions. Write each phrase in the correct column in the chart.

As far as I'm concerned,	It is thought that	Some people say that
In my experience,	. . . is generally considered to be . . .	Speaking for myself,
It is accepted that	Personally, I think	

Personal Opinion	General Opinion

A | Planning. Decide which of the methods you listed on page 123 is best. Follow the steps to make notes for your essay.

Step 1 Make notes for your introduction in the outline.

Step 2 Write your thesis statement.

Step 3 For each topic sentence, write one reason why the method you chose is effective.

Step 4 For each body paragraph, note examples or details that support your topic sentence. Include an example of a personal experience in at least one paragraph.

Step 5 Make notes for your conclusion.

Introduction: _____

_____

Thesis statement: _____

1st body paragraph:

Topic sentence: _____

_____

Examples or details: _____

_____

2nd body paragraph:

Topic sentence: _____

_____

Examples or details: _____

_____

3rd body paragraph:

Topic sentence: _____

_____

Examples or details: _____

_____

Conclusion:

Restatement of thesis: _____

Final thought: _____

B | Draft 1. Use your outline to write a first draft of your essay.

Author Emilie Buchwald once said, "Children are made readers on the laps of their parents." I agree with her statement, and I think that some children very easily begin reading on their own as a result of having been read to by their parents. But, in my experience, it's not always that straightforward. Many children have difficulty with reading comprehension or are not interested in reading because they think it's boring. I believe that to teach these children to read, parents, teachers, and other responsible adults have to make it a point to read aloud books that are interesting to the children and are slightly above the children's reading level.

When books are interesting, children understand that reading can be exciting and, as a result, they pay attention. Excited by the events in a story, children have a purpose for listening as someone reads to them—they need to find out what happens next. That purpose can increase reading comprehension. When children begin reading on their own and are given books that they will enjoy, they have a purpose for reading, which will motivate them to try to understand what they're reading.

Even books without exciting stories can be interesting if children can connect the books to their own lives. Relatable characters and events give children something to discuss after a book is finished. This shows children that books can teach them something. Looking for meaning as they listen along, children begin to learn that reading has value. Traditionally, it was thought that children have to first learn to read, and then read to learn. In other words, children have to learn the sounds of letters first and then learn that the letters can form words with meaning. Personally, I think that it's never too early to start equating reading with learning. As far as I'm concerned, children as young as two or three years old can begin to understand that books can teach them something.

When children start to read by themselves, it can still be helpful to read to them, especially if the books that are read to them are a bit higher than their reading level. To increase vocabulary, children need to hear and read words that they don't know. Confused or puzzled by unfamiliar words, children will push themselves to learn because the words are relevant to the story. When parents or teachers realize that they've just read an unfamiliar word, they should resist explaining the definition right away. Rereading the surrounding sentences slowly, they encourage children to try to use context to guess the meaning of the word, teaching them an important skill they can use throughout their reading lives.

When children are encouraged to see books and stories as tools that can excite them, teach them, and take them to new worlds, they are motivated to read. This motivation goes a long way toward creating strong readers. Reading interesting books that are higher than a child's reading level can help build a strong desire to read and an understanding of what words have to offer. Surfing the Internet, reading information on social networking sites, and clicking on links to read entertaining blog posts, people read more these days than they ever have in the past. In the future, the need for strong reading skills will probably increase. Therefore, understanding the value of reading at a very young age can only benefit children in the future.

Step 1 Underline the thesis statement.

Step 2 Circle the surprising statement, interesting question, quotation, or story in the introduction.

Step 3 Underline the topic sentences of the body paragraphs.

Step 4 Circle each reason in the body paragraphs.

Step 5 Label the features of the conclusion (restatement of thesis, explanation, final thought).

D | **Revising.** Follow steps 1–5 in exercise **C** to analyze your opinion essay.

E | **Peer Evaluation.** Exchange your first draft with a partner and follow these steps.

Step 1 Read your partner's essay and tell him or her one thing that you liked about it.

Step 2 Complete the outline showing the ideas that your partner's essay describes.

Introduction: _____

_____

Thesis statement: _____

1st body paragraph:

Topic sentence: _____

_____

Examples or details: _____

_____

2nd body paragraph:

Topic sentence: _____

_____

Examples or details: _____

_____

3rd body paragraph:

Topic sentence: _____

_____

Examples or details: _____

_____

Conclusion:

Restatement of thesis: _____

Final thought: _____

Step 3 Compare this outline with the one that your partner created in exercise **A** on page 137.

Step 4 The two outlines should be similar. If they aren't, discuss how they differ.

F | Draft 2. Write a second draft of your essay. Use what you learned from the peer evaluation activity and your answers to exercise **D**. Make any other necessary changes.

G | Editing Practice. Read the information in the box and find and correct one mistake with verbal phrases in each sentence (1–5). Then write the letter for the type of mistake you find.

When you use verbal phrases, remember:

- verbal phrases modify nouns, pronouns, or whole clauses.
- to separate a verbal phrase from a clause with a comma.
- you don't need a comma if an infinitive verbal phrase comes at the end of a sentence.

Types of mistakes:

a. no noun, pronoun, or clause after the verbal phrase
b. unnecessary comma
c. missing comma

1. _____ Taking classes every night, learned a lot quickly.

2. _____ You can take private lessons, to learn a new language.

3. _____ Living in a bilingual household I learned Spanish easily.

4. _____ To improve your pronunciation you have to practice.

5. _____ Watching TV in English, learned a lot of natural language.

H | Editing Checklist. Use the checklist to find errors in your second draft.

Editing Checklist	Yes	No
1. Are all the words spelled correctly?		
2. Does every sentence have correct punctuation?		
3. Do your subjects and verbs agree?		
4. Have you used verbal phrases correctly?		
5. Did you vary your phrases for introducing an opinion?		
6. Are your verb tenses correct?		

I | Final Draft. Now use your Editing Checklist to write a third draft of your paper. Make any other necessary changes.

Resources and Development

UNIT

7

ACADEMIC PATHWAYS

Lesson A: Identifying a writer's point of view
Understanding cohesion (II)

Lesson B: Researching and note-taking
Writing an expository essay

◀ A woman in
Iringa, Tanzania,
uses her solar
light to chase
away hyenas.

Think and Discuss

1. What factors are important for a
country's economic development?

2. What resources does your country
have? What resources does it lack?

141

Exploring the Theme

A. Look at the map and key. Then answer the questions.

  1. What regions have the highest concentrations of low-income people? What regions have the highest concentrations of high-income people?

  2. What makes the average incomes of China and India fall into the lower middle-class range?

B. Read the information on development and discuss your answers to the questions.

  1. What does development mean, in terms of economics?

  2. How do developing and developed countries differ?

  3. What is one way to rate a country's level of development?

○ City with population of 10 million or more

0 mi   1000
0 km   1000

MAP DATA: OAK RIDGE NATIONAL LABORATORY
LANDSCAN 2009 (POPULATION DENSITY)

Global
Development

Where and How We Live

The map shows population density; the brightest points are the highest densities. Each country is colored according to its average annual gross national income per capita, using categories established by the World Bank. Some nations—such as economic powerhouses China and India—have an especially wide range of incomes. But as the two most populous countries, both are lower middle class when income is averaged per capita.

LOW INCOME LEVEL	LOWER MIDDLE	UPPER MIDDLE	HIGH
$995 or less a year	$996 to $3,945	$3,946 to $12,195	$12,196 or more
100 1,000 10,000	100 1,000 10,000	100 1,000 10,000	100 1,000 10,000
People per square mile	People per square mile	People per square mile	People per square mile

Defining Development

In economics, **development** is often used to refer to a change from a traditional economy to one based on technology. A traditional economy usually centers on individual survival. Families and small communities often make their own food, clothing, housing, and household goods. The economies of developing countries often rely heavily on agriculture. Developing countries also rely on raw materials, which can be traded to developed countries for finished goods. These raw materials include oil, coal, and timber.

Developed countries have economies that are more diverse. Their economies rely on many different people and organizations performing specialized tasks. Agriculture and raw materials represent only part of the economy of a developed country. Other sectors include manufacturing, banking and finance, and services such as hairdressing and plumbing. This vast economy results in a great variety of goods and services.

One way to rate a country's level of development is by the total value of goods and services the country produces, divided by the number of people in the country. This is called the gross national income (GNI) per capita.

A | Building Vocabulary. Read the following paragraph. Use the context to guess the meanings of the words in **blue**. Then write each word next to its definition (1–6).

For people in developing nations, solar-powered devices can offer several **distinct** advantages. The availability of low-cost solar lamps, for example, means longer working hours—and therefore more employment opportunities—as well as better security at night. In recognition of this move toward solar energy, an organization in Uganda—Solar Sister—is turning local women into solar entrepreneurs. Solar Sister participants sell solar-powered products such as lamps and phone chargers. The women can start with only **rudimentary** business skills, because Solar Sister provides training. In addition, women can start a business with no initial financial **investment**, because Solar Sister provides products for them to sell when they begin. The women can then repay the cost of their starter products once their businesses get going. A successful entrepreneur can make up to $540 in **annual** income. One success story is a Ugandan woman named Grace. **Revenue** from her solar sales business tripled the family income, **thereby** allowing all of her children to attend school.

1. _____: yearly

2. _____: noticeable, important; separate

3. _____: use of money for income or profit

4. _____: money that a company earns

5. _____: basic; not at a high level

6. _____: by this means

▲ A student uses a solar light to study.

B | Building Vocabulary. Complete the definitions (1–6) with the words and phrase from the box. Use a dictionary to help you.

> denied   evolutionary   military intervention
>
> minority   orientation   tensions

1. The _____ of a thing is its position relative to something else.

2. _____ occurs when armed forces—such as an army—go into a place to solve a conflict.

3. If you are _____ something, you cannot do it or have it.

4. "_____" describes a process of gradual change and development.

5. _____ are feelings that occur where there is a possibility of violence or conflict.

6. A _____ is a smaller number or part of things in a larger group.

C | Using Vocabulary. Answer the questions. Share your ideas with a partner.

1. What kinds of **tensions** do you hear about currently in the news?

2. What do you think is the minimum **annual** income that people in your country need to live well?

3. Do you think **military intervention** can ever be the best way to resolve a political conflict? Why, or why not?

Word Partners

Use **tension** with verbs, nouns, and adjectives: (v.): **ease** tension, **relieve** tension; (n.): **source of** tension; (adj.): **racial** tension, **ethnic** tension

D | Brainstorming. Discuss your answers to these questions in small groups.

What do you know about Africa? What comes to mind when you think about Africa?

E | Predicting. Look at the image on pages 146–147. Then read the first and last sentences of each paragraph of the reading passage (pages 146–151). Discuss your answers to these questions (1–3) with a partner. Check your ideas as you read the rest of the passage.

1. Describe the location and geographical orientation of the continent of Africa. How does its orientation appear to be different from that of other continents?

2. What topics will the article probably discuss? Geography? History? Both geography and history?

3. Will the article discuss problems? Solutions? Both problems and solutions?

THE SHAPE OF
AFRICA
by Jared Diamond

The hope for Africa's future lies with its abundant human and natural resources.

track **2-02**

A

ASK SOMEONE TO TELL YOU quickly what they associate with Africa and the answers you'll get will probably range from "cradle of humankind" and "big animals" to "poverty" and "tribalism." How did one continent come to embody such extremes?

Geography and history go a long way toward providing the explanations. Geographically, Africa resembles a bulging sandwich. The sole continent to span both the north and south temperate zones,[1] it has

B

a thick tropical core lying between one thin temperate zone in the north and another in the south. That simple geographic reality explains a great deal about Africa today.

As to its human history, this is the place where some seven million years ago the **evolutionary** lines of apes and protohumans[2] diverged. It remained the only continent our ancestors inhabited until around two million years ago, when *Homo erectus* expanded out of Africa into Europe and Asia. Over the next 1.5 million years, the populations of those three continents followed such different evolutionary courses that they became **distinct** species. Europe's became the Neandertals, Asia's remained *Homo erectus*, but Africa's evolved into our

C

own species, *Homo sapiens*. Sometime between 100,000 and 50,000 years ago, our African ancestors underwent some further profound change. Whether it was the development of complex speech or something else, such as a change in brain wiring, we aren't sure. Whatever it was, it transformed those early *Homo sapiens* into what paleoanthropologists[3] call "behaviorally modern" *Homo sapiens*. Those people, probably with brains similar to our own, expanded again into Europe and Asia. Once there, they exterminated or replaced or interbred with Neandertals and Asia's hominins and became the dominant human species throughout the world.

[1] **Temperate zones** are areas between the tropics and the polar circle.
[2] A **protohuman** is an early human ancestor.
[3] **Paleoanthropologists** are scientists who study human fossils.

D In effect, Africans enjoyed not just one but three huge head starts over humans on other continents. That makes Africa's economic struggles today, compared with the successes of other continents, particularly puzzling. It's the opposite of what one would expect from the runner first off the block. Here again, geography and history give us answers.

E It turns out that the rules of the competitive race among the world's humans changed radically about 10,000 years ago, with the origins of agriculture. The domestication of wild plants and animals meant our ancestors could grow their own food instead of having to hunt or gather it in the wild. That allowed people to settle in permanent villages, to increase their populations, and to feed specialists—inventors, soldiers, and kings—who did not produce food. With domestication came other advances, including the first metal tools, writing, and state societies.

F The problem is that only a tiny **minority** of wild plants and animals lend themselves to domestication, and those few are concentrated in about half a dozen parts of the world. As every schoolchild learns, the world's earliest and most productive farming arose in the Fertile Crescent of southwestern Asia, where wheat, barley, sheep, cattle, and goats were domesticated. While those plants and animals spread east and west in Eurasia, in Africa they were stopped by the continent's north-south **orientation**. Crops and livestock tend to spread much more slowly from north to south than from east to west because different latitudes require adaptation to different climates, seasonalities, day lengths, and diseases. Africa's own native plant species—sorghum, oil palm, coffee, millets, and yams—weren't domesticated until thousands of years after Asia and Europe had agriculture. And Africa's geography kept oil palm, yams, and other crops of equatorial Africa from spreading into southern Africa's temperate zone. While South Africa today boasts[4] the continent's richest agricultural lands, the crops grown there are mostly northern temperate crops, such as wheat and grapes, brought directly on ships by European colonists. Those same crops never succeeded in spreading south through the thick tropical core of Africa.

[4] To **boast** is to possess a feature that is a source of pride.

▼ Betsileo woman carrying a bundle of rice in Madagascar

▲ Botswana's San people, or Bushmen, are some of the world's last surviving hunter-gatherers.

The domesticated sheep and cattle of Fertile Crescent origins took about 5,000 years to spread from the Mediterranean down to the southern tip of Africa. The continent's own native animals—with the exception of guinea fowl and possibly donkeys and one breed of cattle—proved impossible to domesticate. History might have turned out differently if African armies, fed by barnyard-giraffe meat and backed by waves of cavalry[5] mounted on huge rhinos, had swept into Europe to overrun its mutton-fed soldiers mounted on puny horses. That this didn't happen was no fault of the Africans; it was because of the kinds of wild animals available to them.

Ironically, the long human presence in Africa is probably the reason the continent's species of big animals survive today. African animals co-evolved with humans for millions of years, as human hunting prowess gradually progressed from the **rudimentary** skills of our early ancestors. That gave the animals time to learn a healthy fear of man and, with it, a healthy avoidance of human hunters. In contrast, North and South America and Australia were settled by humans only within the last tens of thousands of years. To the misfortune of the big animals of those continents, the first humans they encountered were already fully modern people, with modern brains and hunting skills. Most of those animals—woolly mammoths, saber-toothed cats, and in Australia marsupials[6] as big as rhinoceroses—disappeared soon after humans arrived. Entire species may have been exterminated before they had time to learn to beware of hunters.

Unfortunately, the long human presence in Africa also encouraged something else to thrive—diseases. The continent has a well-deserved reputation for having spawned some of our nastiest ones: malaria, yellow fever, East African sleeping sickness, and AIDS. These and many other human illnesses arose when microbes causing disease in animals crossed species lines to evolve into a human disease. For a microbe already adapted to one species, to adapt to another can be difficult and require a lot of evolutionary time. Much more time has been available in Africa, cradle of humankind, than in any other part of the planet. That's half the answer to Africa's disease burden; the other half is that the animal species most closely related to humans—those whose microbes required the least adaptation to jump species—are the African great apes and monkeys.

[5] A **cavalry** is a group of soldiers who ride horses.
[6] **Marsupials** are animals such as kangaroos. Female marsupials carry their babies in pouches on their bellies.

Africa continues to be shaped in other ways by its long history and its geography. Of mainland Africa's ten richest countries—the only ones with **annual** per capita gross domestic products over $3,500— nine lie partly or entirely within its temperate zones: Egypt, Libya, Tunisia, Algeria, and Morocco in the north; and Swaziland, South Africa, Botswana, and **J** Namibia in the south. Gabon is Africa's only tropical country to make the list. In addition, nearly a third of the countries of mainland Africa (15 out of 47) are landlocked, and the only African river navigable[7] from the ocean for long distances inland is the Nile. Since waterways provide the cheapest way to transport cumbersome[8] goods, geography again thwarts Africa's progress.

K All these factors can lead to the question: "Is the continent, or at least its big tropical core, doomed eternally to wars, poverty, and devastating diseases?"

I'd answer, "Absolutely not." On my own visits to Africa, I've been struck by how harmoniously ethnic groups live together in many countries—far better than they do in many other parts of the globe. **Tensions** arise in Africa, as they do elsewhere, when people see no other way out of poverty except to fight their neighbors for dwindling resources. But many areas of Africa have an abundance of resources: The rivers of central Africa are great generators of hydroelectric power; the big animals are a major source of ecotourism **revenue** in eastern and southern Africa; and the forests in the wetter regions, if managed and logged sustainably, would be renewable and lucrative[9] sources of income.

[7] A **navigable** river is wide enough for a boat to travel along safely.
[8] If something is **cumbersome**, it is large and heavy and therefore difficult to carry or handle.
[9] A **lucrative** activity, job, or business is very profitable.

> " History might have turned out differently if African armies, fed by barnyard-giraffe meat and backed by waves of cavalry mounted on huge rhinos, had swept into Europe . . . "

As for Africa's health problems, they can be greatly alleviated with the right planning and funding. Within the past half century, several formerly poor countries in Asia recognized that tropical diseases were a major drain on their economies. By investing in public health measures, they have successfully curbed those diseases, and the increased health of their people has led to far healthier economies. Within Africa itself, some international mining and oil companies have been funding successful public health programs throughout their concession areas[10] because they realized that protecting the health of their workers was an excellent business **investment** for them.

What's the best case for Africa's future? If the continent can overcome its health problems and the corruption that plagues many of its governments and institutions, then it could take advantage of today's globalized, technological world in much the same way that China and India are now doing. Technology could give Africa the connections that its geography, particularly its rivers, long **denied** it. Nearly half of all African countries are English speaking, an advantage in trade relations, and an educated, English-speaking workforce could well attract service jobs to many African countries.

If Africa is to head into a bright future, outside investment will continue to be needed, at least for a time. The cost of perpetual aid to or **military intervention** in Africa is thousands of times more expensive than solving health problems and supporting local development, **thereby** heading off [11] conflicts. Not only Africans but the rest of us will be healthier and safer if Africa's nations increasingly take their places as peaceful and prospering members of the world community.

[10] A **concession area** is a place where someone is given the right to sell a product or run a business.
[11] If you **head off** an event, you keep it from happening.

▼ Cape Town Stadium, seen here from Table Mountain, was built for the 2010 Soccer World Cup and has become a symbol of modern Africa.

A | Identifying Main Ideas. Skim the reading again. Write the correct paragraph letter (B, C, D, E, G, H) next to each main idea (1–7).

1. ____ The co-evolution of animals and humans affected the survival of some species in Africa.

2. ____ Humans have been in Africa for a very long time.

3. ____ Africa's geographical orientation affected the spread of agriculture on the continent.

4. ____ It's a mystery why the long human history of Africa hasn't been an advantage.

5. ____ Africa's geographic location explains the extremes that exist on the continent.

6. ____ The development of agriculture impacts a culture.

7. ____ Animal domestication took a long time to spread across Africa.

B | Identifying Main Ideas. Complete the main idea statements for paragraphs I, J, and K. Then write the main ideas of paragraphs L, M, and N using the paraphrasing strategies you learned in Unit 4.

1. Paragraph I: The long human presence in Africa led to _____.

2. Paragraph J: The richest countries in Africa lie in _____.

3. Paragraph K: Africa has hope because of _____.

4. Paragraph L: _____

_____

5. Paragraph M: _____

_____

6. Paragraph N: _____

_____

C | Critical Thinking: Identifying Chronology. Find these events in paragraph C. Put each event (a–f) in the correct place in the time line.

a. "behaviorally modern" *Homo sapiens* appear in Africa
b. *Homo erectus* evolves into three distinct species: Neandertals in Europe, *Homo erectus* in Asia, *Homo sapiens* in Africa
c. apes and protohumans split
d. *Homo erectus* moves to Europe and Asia
e. *Homo sapiens* wipe out Neandertals and *Homo erectus* and become dominant species
f. *Homo sapiens* move into Europe and Asia

D | Identifying Key Details. Write answers to the questions.

1. What are the "head starts" that Diamond refers to in paragraph D?

   _____

   _____

2. What are some effects of the development of agriculture?

   _____

   _____

3. What blocked the spread of agriculture in Africa?

   _____

   _____

4. Why did many animal species survive in Africa, unlike other places such as Australia?

   _____

   _____

5. Why is the proximity to great apes and monkeys a problem in Africa?

   _____

   _____

6. What two geographical conditions affect the wealth of Africa?

   _____

   _____

7. How does Diamond describe the potential of Africa's resources?

   _____

   _____

8. What actions may give Africa a better future?

   _____

   _____

E | Identifying Meaning from Context. Find and underline the following words and phrases in the reading passage on pages 146–151. Use context to help you identify the meaning of each word or phrase. Match each word or phrase with its definition.

1. _____ Paragraph B: **go a long way toward**

2. _____ Paragraph D: **head starts**

3. _____ Paragraph F: **lend themselves to**

4. _____ Paragraph I: **spawned**

5. _____ Paragraph J: **landlocked**

6. _____ Paragraph K: **struck by**

7. _____ Paragraph L: **a (major) drain on**

8. _____ Paragraph M: **plagues**

a. a use of something such as resources that most people feel is not a good use

b. caused to happen

c. surrounded by other countries and not having access to bodies of water

d. help a great deal

e. advantages in a competition

f. continually causes problems

g. impressed by

h. are suitable for, or adapt easily to

CT Focus: Identifying Point of View

It's important to identify a writer's attitude, or **point of view**, toward his or her topic in order to fully understand the main ideas. Look for clues to the point of view in how the writer presents advantages and disadvantages. Does one receive more weight than the other? Look also at language use. Point of view can be indicated directly through word choice—for example, by the use of words and expressions with positive or negative connotations.

F | Critical Thinking: Analyzing a Writer's Point of View. Analyze Diamond's point of view by discussing your answers to the following questions.

1. In paragraph K, Diamond answers his own question, "Absolutely not." Why did Diamond choose to add *absolutely* to his answer?

2. What aspects of Africa today does Diamond describe in paragraph K? What word does Diamond use to describe the way ethnic groups live together in Africa?

3. What word does Diamond use to describe the number of resources in Africa? Why did he use this word instead of *a lot of*?

4. In general, how does Diamond describe Africa's future in paragraphs K–M? In a positive way or in a negative way? How do you know?

5. What is Diamond's point of view overall? Is his attitude about Africa's future basically optimistic or pessimistic?

A piece of writing has cohesion when all of its parts are connected logically and flow smoothly from one idea the next. In Unit 1, you saw how writers use pronouns, demonstratives, and synonyms. Another cohesive device is the repetition of key words.

Often, writers use key words early in a piece of writing when they are stating the thesis. Then they refer to the key words later on as they develop the supporting information for their thesis. This helps the reader to follow the flow of ideas. The references to the key words may be repetitions or paraphrases.

Example of a thesis for an essay on problems and solutions in the state of California:

> *California's economy has been affected by <u>population growth</u> and <u>taxation policies</u>.*
>   **key phrase**   **key phrase**

Example of repetition of a key word or phrase in a body paragraph:

> *Dramatic <u>population growth</u> in the 2000s has led to . . .*
>   **repetition**

Example of paraphrasing of a key word or phrase in a body paragraph:

> *The <u>reduction of property taxes</u> in the 1970s had a long-range effect on . . .*
>   **paraphrase**

A | **Analyzing.** Answer the questions to analyze the use of key word repetition in "The Shape of Africa."

1. Complete the key words in Diamond's thesis.

   Africa has been shaped by its _____ and _____ .

2. Where does he repeat or paraphrase these key words? List examples from the text. Note the paragraph where you find each one.

   the long human presence (H)

B | **Critical Thinking: Evaluating.** Discuss these questions with a partner.

Does the organization of Diamond's article, especially the use of repetition and paraphrasing, help you to understand his ideas? Why, or why not?

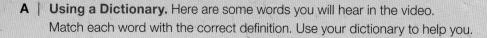

The Encroaching Desert

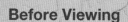

Before Viewing

A | Using a Dictionary. Here are some words you will hear in the video. Match each word with the correct definition. Use your dictionary to help you.

▲ A scorching sun casts long shadows as camels cross salt flats in Djibouti.

| hectare | monsoon | nomadic | sterile |

1. _____: not able to produce living things, such as plants

2. _____: a measurement of area, equal to 2.471 acres or 10,000 square meters

3. _____: moving from place to place; not having a permanent home

4. _____: seasonal, heavy rainfall

B | Thinking Ahead. What do you remember from Unit 1 about *desertification*? Work with a partner to write an explanation of it in your own words.

_____

_____

_____

While Viewing

Read questions 1–4. Think about the answers as you view the video.

1. What was the Sahara desert like 4,000 years ago?

2. What role did monsoon rains play in the Sahel in the past?

3. On what other continent is desertification a problem?

4. What is happening to 5–6 million hectares of farmland every year?

After Viewing

A | Discuss your answers to questions 1–4 above with a partner.

B | Critical Thinking: Synthesizing. How might Jared Diamond explain the role desertification plays in the conditions that exist in Africa today?

GOAL: Writing an Expository Essay

In this lesson, you are going to plan, write, revise, and edit an essay on the following topic: **Choose a country or region and explain how it has been affected by its history and geography.**

A | Brainstorming. Make a list of two or three countries or regions that interest you. What do you know about key events in their history and important aspects of their geography? List facts in the chart. Then select the country or region you will research.

Countries/Regions	History	Geography

B | Vocabulary for Writing. The words and phrases below can be useful when writing about geography and history. Find them in the reading passage on pages 146–151, and use context to guess their meanings. Then match each word or phrase to its definition.

1. _____: **embody** (paragraph A)

2. _____: **span** (paragraph B)

3. _____: **underwent** (paragraph C)

4. _____: **concentrated in** (paragraph F)

5. _____: **be shaped in** (paragraph J)

6. _____: **per capita gross domestic products** (paragraph J)

a. to extend over a large area

b. experienced; suffered (from)

c. to be influenced in

d. to be a symbol of

e. the economic output of a country by person

f. located in one place instead of being distributed

Free Writing. Write for five minutes about one aspect of the country or region you chose in exercise **A**, such as its location or its resources. Try to use some of the words and phrases from exercise **B**.

C | Read the information in the box. Then write quotes and paraphrases using a different reporting verb and phrase in each sentence.

Language for Writing: Referring to Sources

When you use other people's ideas in your writing, you either quote them directly or you paraphrase them. Try to paraphrase as much as possible, but use direct quotations when the original words are particularly effective. Use the following words and phrases to refer to sources.

According to Diamond, *"The long human presence in Africa is probably the reason the continent's species of big animals survive today."*

As Diamond says, *"The long human presence in Africa is probably the reason the continent's species of big animals survive today."*

Diamond says that *"the long human presence in Africa is probably the reason the continent's species of big animals survive today."*

Diamond says that *the fact that humans have been in Africa for a very long time probably explains why many animal species still exist on the continent.*

It's common to use *that* after reporting verbs in academic writing. Note that when you use *that* in a quote, it must fit grammatically into the sentence.

Vary your style by using different reporting verbs, such as the following:
says, states, claims, believes, explains, points out, suggests, reports, concludes, argues.

Choose a reporting verb that matches the meaning you intend. For example, if you are reporting on research, you might say, "X concludes that." If you are reporting on a persuasive idea, you might say, "X argues that." If you are reporting on an opinion, you might use "X thinks/believes/feels that."

1. Write a quote that answers this question: What may have happened to the large animals that disappeared in Australia and North and South America? (paragraph H)

_____

_____

2. Write a quote that expresses Diamond's opinion on how people get along with each other in Africa. (paragraph K)

_____

_____

3. Rewrite your paraphrase of the main idea of paragraph L (page 152) using a reporting verb.

_____

4. Rewrite your paraphrase of the main idea of paragraph M (page 152) using a reporting verb.

_____

Writing Skill: Researching and Note-taking

When researching information online for an essay, you may need to choose and evaluate sources quickly and efficiently. You will also need to note the most relevant information. Use these tips to make your research and note-taking more effective.

Researching

- Limit your search results by using precise key words with quotation marks around them.

- Scan the URLs in your search results to quickly eliminate sites that don't appear to be relevant.

- Avoid encyclopedia sites as your main source, when possible. You will write a better essay if you use original sources. However, encyclopedia sites may be a good place to find original sources—check the References section at the end of each article.

- When you go to a source site, preview the content: Read the title and the subheads, look at the pictures, and read the captions. As you preview, ask yourself: Is the site trustworthy? Is the information accurate? Is it current? Is the information thorough?

Note-taking

- Avoid plagiarism by having index cards handy or a note-taking document open while you are doing online research. When you find information that is useful, write the ideas in your own words. Never cut and paste text from websites!

- In your notes, include all correct source information: the correct names of people and the publications you will refer to in your essay.

- For ideas that you will quote directly, write the source of the quotation and the exact words that you will quote.

- Label your notes with a *P* for information that you have paraphrased and a *Q* for information you have quoted.

D | **Critical Thinking: Researching.** Work with a partner. Look at the following research questions and discuss your answers to these questions: What key words should you use for an online search? What types of websites would give you the best information?

1. What are some ways to improve agricultural production in Africa?

2. What languages are spoken in Africa?

3. What are some examples of how outside aid has helped Africa?

E | Critical Thinking: Note-Taking. Compare the following notes on an original text. Which is the better version? Why? Share your answer with a partner.

The impacts of slavery on Africa are widespread and diverse. Computerized calculations have projected that if there had been no slave trade, the population of Africa would have been 50 million instead of 25 million in 1850.

— From National Geographic Encyclopedia:
   http://education.nationalgeographic.com/education/encyclopedia/

a. Slavery has had a huge impact on Africa. There would have been 50 million inhabitants in Africa instead of only 25 million in 1850 if there had been no slave trade.

b. Slavery had several damaging effects on Africa; for example, it reduced the population by 50 percent in the 19th century.

F | Critical Thinking: Applying. Research information on one of the countries or regions you chose in exercise **A**. Take notes on the following points.

1. Find background information on the country or region. What is it like today?

_____
_____
_____
_____

2. Find out about the geography of the country or region. How does its geography affect its current situation? Find out where it is located, what its climate is like, what its main resources are, and so on.

_____
_____
_____
_____

3. Find out about the history of the country or region. What are the key events? How does its history affect its current situation?

_____
_____
_____
_____

A | Planning. Use your research notes to plan your essay. Follow the steps.

Step 1 Choose three aspects of the geography and history of the country / region that you want to discuss. Write a thesis statement in the outline.

Step 2 Write a topic sentence for each of your body paragraphs. Remember to reflect your key concepts in your topic sentences.

Step 3 For each body paragraph, write two to three examples or details that explain the ideas in your topic sentences.

Step 4 Note some ideas for an introduction and a conclusion for your essay.

Thesis statement:
What are three key aspects of the country's/region's geography/history that affect the way it is today?

_____

1st body paragraph: one aspect of its geography/history

Topic sentence: _____

_____

Explanation and examples: _____

_____

_____

2nd body paragraph: another aspect of its geography/history

Topic sentence: _____

_____

Explanation and examples: _____

_____

_____

3rd body paragraph: third aspect of its geography/history

Topic sentence: _____

_____

Explanation and examples: _____

_____

_____

Ideas for introduction and conclusion: _____

_____

B | Draft 1. Use your outline to write a first draft of your essay.

Singapore is a collection of small islands in Southeast Asia. The majority of the population is concentrated on the mainland, a diamond-shaped island 30 miles (49 km) wide and 15.5 miles (25 km) long. Singapore boasts the world's largest concentration of millionaires, is culturally diverse, and frequently ranks in the top ten in work- and personal-life satisfaction surveys. What makes Singapore the place that it is today? Its geographical location, its lack of natural resources (especially fresh water), and its recent immigration history have all played a part in shaping this small island nation.

Thanks to its geography, trade is one of the most important aspects of Singapore's economy. The country lies to the south of Malaysia, from which it is separated by a narrow body of water called the Johor Strait. Its southern coast is on the Singapore Strait, which separates it from Indonesia. Its advantageous location made it a key stopping-off point for ships traveling from Asia to Europe. As a result, Singapore became an important center for international trade. In the 1970s, the government invested in building ports along the coast. This made it even easier for ships to come and go. Today, the Port of Singapore is one of the busiest in the world. This has helped Singapore to become the 14th largest exporter and the 15th largest importer in the world.

The lack of natural resources, especially fresh water, has also shaped Singapore. Having a rain forest climate, Singapore receives over 90 inches of rainfall a year. However, because it has little land to retain the water, the supply of fresh drinking water for Singapore's citizens is very limited. As a result, Singapore must import water from nearby countries. In addition, the country has built water-recycling and desalination plants. Water-recycling plants transform wastewater into drinking water, and desalination plants make use of the abundant seawater that surrounds the island. According to the Public Utilities Board (PUB), Singapore's national water agency, current and planned plants will meet up to 55 percent of the demand for fresh water by 2060.

Singapore's recent history of immigration goes a long way toward explaining its rich cultural diversity. For many years, the government of Singapore had liberal immigration policies. The country needed foreign workers partly due to its low birthrate: there are only .78 births per woman, which is below the replacement rate of 2.1. By 2005, 40 percent of the population was made up of residents from other parts of Asia, North America, and Europe. Although there has been some opposition to these liberal immigration policies in recent history, many experts believe that immigration is necessary to maintain a strong workforce and to offset an aging population. In a *Forbes* magazine interview, investor and Singapore resident Jim Rogers argued that if Singapore cannot get enough labor through immigration, inflation may result, with an overall detrimental effect on the country's economy. As Rogers pointed out, "Every country in history that has a backlash against foreigners is going to go into decline."

As with many countries, Singapore has been shaped by its geography and history. Since gaining its independence from Malaysia in 1965, the tiny city-state has gone from a poor trading port to one of the wealthiest states in the world. And it shows: High-rise condos and skyscrapers dominate the landscape, and shoppers peruse the latest designer goods in its many upscale malls and boutiques. Although Singapore is a small country with a declining birthrate and few natural resources, its advantageous location in the heart of Southeast Asia will continue to make it attractive to immigrants, tourists, and investors alike.

Step 1   Underline the thesis statement and circle the key words.

Step 2   Underline the topic sentences of the body paragraphs. Does the order of the body paragraphs reflect the order of the ideas in the thesis?

Step 3   Circle the key words in the topic sentences. Do they reflect the key words in the thesis statement?

Step 4   What details in the body paragraphs does the writer use to develop the key concepts in each of the topic sentences?

Step 5   Where has the writer referred to sources? Which reporting verbs and phrases has the writer used?

D | Revising. Follow the steps in exercise **C** to analyze your own essay.

E | Peer Evaluation. Exchange your first draft with a partner and follow these steps.

Step 1   Read your partner's essay and tell him or her one thing that you liked about it.

Step 2   Complete the outline showing the ideas that your partner's essay describes.

Thesis statement:

What are three key aspects of geography/history that affect the way the country/region is today?

_____

1st body paragraph: one aspect of its geography/history

Topic sentence: _____

_____

Explanation and examples: _____

_____

_____

2nd body paragraph: another aspect of its geography/history

Topic sentence: _____

_____

Explanation and examples: _____

_____

_____

3rd body paragraph: third aspect of its geography/history

Topic s entence: _____

_____

Explanation and examples: _____

_____

_____

Ideas for introduction and conclusion: _____

_____

Step 3 Compare this outline with the one that your partner created in exercise **A** on page 161.

Step 4 The two outlines should be similar. If they aren't, discuss how they differ.

F | **Draft 2.** Write a second draft of your essay. Use what you learned from the peer evaluation activity and your answers to exercise **D**. Make any other necessary changes.

G | **Editing Practice.** Read the information in the box. Then find and correct one mistake with quotes or paraphrases in each sentence (1–4).

When you refer to sources, remember to:

- use correct punctuation. With quotes, use quotation marks and a comma to separate a person's exact words from the rest of the sentence. Use a comma after the phrase that includes *According to*.
- make sure that sentences referring to sources are grammatical. For example, do not use *that* with "As X says ~~that~~ . . ."

---

1. Susan Sontag said that To photograph is to confer importance.
2. According to Griffiths photography has influenced our notion of what is beautiful.
3. Diamond asks, What's the best case for Africa's future?"
4. As Kolbert says that, "Probably the most obvious way humans are altering the planet is by building cities."

H | **Editing Checklist.** Use the checklist to find errors in your second draft.

Editing Checklist	Yes	No
1. Are all the words spelled correctly?		
2. Does every sentence have correct punctuation?		
3. Do your subjects and verbs agree?		
4. Have you used reporting verbs and phrases correctly?		
5. Are your verb tenses correct?		

I | **Final Draft.** Now use your Editing Checklist to write a third draft of your essay. Make any other necessary changes.

Living Longer

ACADEMIC PATHWAYS

Lesson A: Predicting a conclusion
            Asking questions as you read
Lesson B: Planning a research paper
            Writing an argumentative research paper

UNIT

8

Think and Discuss

1. What daily habits can contribute to good health?

2. How do you think a person's genes can affect their health?

▲ An 89-year-old fisherman from
Okinawa Island, Japan, shows
off his muscles.

165

Look at the map and the chart, and read the information below. Then discuss the questions.

1. What are the main causes of death in North America and Europe?

2. Where in the world are communicable diseases and injuries the main causes of death?

3. What is the life expectancy in your country? What are the main causes of death there?

4. Why do the main causes of death differ around the world?

5. How does income relate to life expectancy?

Causes of Mortality

In the developing world, communicable diseases—such as HIV/AIDS and cholera—are the most common cause of unnatural death. In the world's poorest countries, and particularly in sub-Saharan Africa, a lack of adequate health care and an overabundance of infectious diseases, parasites, and malaria cut lives short. In wealthier, more developed countries, people have more access to health care and nutritious food sources, and they live longer as a result. People in these countries most often die of noncontagious diseases such as diabetes, heart disease, and cancer.

Comparing Income and Life Expectancy

Life expectancy refers to the length of time a typical person is expected to live. In Europe, Central Asia, and North America, high incomes result in longevity, with the average person living for almost 80 years. The area of the world with the lowest income is also the area with the shortest life expectancy. The average life expectancy in sub-Saharan Africa is just over 40 years.

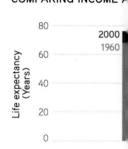

COMPARING INCOME A

ASIA

AUSTRALIA

Cause-specific mortality

Communicable diseases

More

More

Injuries ← More → Noncommunicable diseases

No data available

CY

$5,866
$1,317

$7,161
$3,459

$5,525
$1,935

$32,880
$12,380

$2,346
$892

$1,573
$1,470

ast Asia
d Pacific

Latin America
and the Caribbean

Middle East
and North Africa

North
America

South
Asia

Sub-Saharan
Africa

A | Building Vocabulary. Read the following paragraphs about losing weight. Use the context to guess the meanings of the words and phrase in **blue**. Then write the correct word or phrase to complete each sentence (1–7).

When people want to lose weight, they often skip meals and try to eat smaller amounts of food. They're usually hungry as a result, but it seems like the logical thing to do. Eating and losing weight seem to be two **contradictory** ideas. However, studies show that eating when you're hungry can actually help you lose weight, and, **conversely**, skipping meals can make you gain weight. Why? We have **mechanisms** in our bodies that let us know when we're hungry and when we're full. "Overhunger" can interfere with those mechanisms, and research shows that when people skip a meal and let themselves be overly hungry, they tend to eat more than they need to at their next meal.

The **implication** of this research isn't that you can eat anything you want when you're hungry and still lose 10 pounds; you also need to embrace certain dietary **restrictions**. For example, maintain a low intake of fats and simple carbohydrates such as white bread and pastries. Instead, eat lean proteins and plenty of fruits and vegetables. It's also important to be aware of what you eat. Write down everything you eat—and when you eat it—in a food diary. That way, you can easily **reconstruct** your food intake. Doing so can help you **gain insight into** what is making you gain weight or what is keeping you from losing weight.

1. If two or more facts, ideas, or statements are _____, they state or imply that opposite things are true.

2. You say "_____" to indicate that the situation you are about to describe is the opposite or reverse of the one you have just described.

3. If you _____ a complex situation or problem, you gain an accurate and deep understanding of it.

4. The _____ of a statement, an event, or situation is what it suggests is the case.

5. If you _____ an event that happened in the past, you try to get a complete understanding of it by combining a lot of small pieces of information.

6. You can refer to things that limit what you can do as _____.

7. A(n) _____ is a process or system that enables something to take place.

Word Link

struct = to build:
con**struct**, de**struct**ive, in**struct**, recon**struct**, **struct**ure

B | Building Vocabulary. Complete the definitions (1–5) with the words from the box. Use a dictionary to help you.

| distinction | intact | outnumbers | ratio | unification |

1. _____ is the process by which two or more countries join together and become one country.

Word Link

uni = one:
unification, **uni**form, **uni**fy, **uni**lateral, **uni**on, **uni**sex

2. If one group _____ another, the first group has more people or things in it than the second group.

3. If something has a _____ , it has a particular importance or quality.

4. Something that is _____ is complete and has not been damaged or changed.

5. A(n) _____ is a relationship between two things in numbers or amounts.

C | Using Vocabulary. Answer the questions. Share your ideas with a partner.

1. What are some common dietary **restrictions** that people have? Which ones are voluntary?

2. In your regular diet, do healthy foods **outnumber** unhealthy foods, or vice versa?

3. What do you think is the **ratio** of vegetarians to non-vegetarians in your country?

D | Brainstorming. Discuss your answers to these questions in small groups.

1. What are some factors that can affect a person's life expectancy?

2. What do you think are the most important factors that influence life expectancy?

E | Predicting. Skim the reading passage and look at the photos on pages 171–177. Circle the aspects of longevity that you think the passage will discuss.

genetics	lifestyles	diet	friends
family relationships	community	happiness	socializing
scientific research	luck		

F | Critical Thinking: Predicting a Conclusion. Read paragraphs A–C of the reading passage on pages 171–177. Then write answers to the questions. Check your predictions as you read the rest of the passage.

1. What do you think Passarino and Berardelli were trying to determine?

_____

2. What do you think they discovered?

_____

CT Focus

As you read, try to **predict the author's conclusion**. Re-evaluate your prediction as you read. Thinking ahead will help give more meaning to the information you read.

Reading Skill: Asking Questions as You Read

Asking yourself questions as you read can give you a deeper understanding of the information in the text. It can also help you make inferences about the writer's intent. Engaging with a text by asking questions is almost like having a conversation with the writer.

As you read, predict answers to your questions. Note the answers that you discover as you progress through a text. For example, after reading paragraph A of the reading on page 172, you might ask, "Why are Passarino and Berardelli going to Molochio?" You might predict that they are going there to learn about the culture, to talk to a centenarian, or to learn what it's like to be a centenarian. After reading paragraph B, you learn that the two men are going to talk with centenarian Salvatore Caruso. Then you might ask, "Why do they want to talk to Caruso?"

A | **Asking Questions as You Read.** As you read the passage on pages 171–177, complete the chart.

Paragraphs	Information That You Learned or That Surprised You	Your Questions	Possible Answers to Your Questions	Answers Given Later in the Text
A–D		Why are Passarino and Berardelli going to Molochio? Why do they want to talk to centenarians?		
E–H				
I–K				
L–M				
N–P				

Beyond 100

by Stephen S. Hall

▲ An 83-year-old woman practices yoga in Solana Beach, California.

Our genes harbor many secrets to a long and healthy life. And now scientists are beginning to uncover them.

track 2-03

ON A CRISP JANUARY MORNING, with snow topping the distant Aspromonte mountains and oranges ripening on the nearby trees, Giuseppe Passarino guided his silver minivan up a curving mountain road into the hinterlands of Calabria, mainland Italy's southernmost region. As the road climbed through fruit and olive groves, Passarino, a geneticist at the University of Calabria, chatted with his colleague Maurizio Berardelli, a geriatrician. They were headed for the small village of Molochio, which had the **distinction** of numbering four centenarians— and four 99-year-olds—among its 2,000 inhabitants.

A

Soon after, they found Salvatore Caruso warming his 106-year-old bones in front of a roaring fire in his home on the outskirts of the town. Known in local dialect as "U' Raggiuneri, the Accountant," Caruso was calmly reading an article about the end of the world in an Italian version of a supermarket tabloid.[1] A framed copy of his birth record, dated November 2, 1905, stood on the fireplace mantle.

B

Caruso told the researchers he was in good health, and his memory seemed prodigiously **intact**. He recalled the death of his father in 1913, when Salvatore was a schoolboy; how his mother and brother had nearly died during the great influenza pandemic of 1918–19; how he'd been dismissed from his army unit in 1925 after accidentally falling and breaking his leg in two places. When Berardelli leaned forward and asked Caruso how he had achieved his remarkable longevity, the centenarian said with an impish smile, "*No Bacco, no tabacco, no Venere*—No drinking, no smoking, no women." He added that he'd eaten mostly figs and beans while growing up and hardly ever any red meat.

C

Passarino and Berardelli heard much the same story from 103-year-old Domenico Romeo—who described his diet as "*poco, ma tutto*—a little bit, but of everything"—and 104-year-old Maria Rosa Caruso,

D

who, despite failing health, regaled[2] her visitors with a lively version of a song about the local patron saint.[3]

On the ride back to the laboratory in Cosenza, Berardelli remarked, "They often say they prefer to eat only fruits and vegetables."

E

"They preferred fruit and vegetables," Passarino said drily, "because that's all they had."

F

Although eating sparingly may have been less a choice than an involuntary circumstance of poverty in places like early 20th-century Calabria, decades of research have suggested that a severely restricted diet is connected to long life. Lately, however, this theory has fallen on hard scientific times. Several recent studies have undermined the link between longevity and caloric **restriction**.

G

In any case, Passarino was more interested in the centenarians themselves than in what they had eaten during their lifetimes. In a field historically marred[4] by exaggerated claims and dubious entrepreneurs hawking[5] unproven elixirs,[6] scientists studying longevity have begun using powerful genomic technologies, basic molecular research, and, most important, data on small, genetically isolated communities of people to **gain** increased **insight into** the maladies of old age and how they might be avoided. In Calabria, Ecuador, Hawaii, and even in the Bronx, studies are turning up molecules and chemical pathways that may ultimately help everyone reach an advanced age in good, even vibrant, health.

H

---

[1] A **tabloid** is a newspaper that has small pages, short articles, and a lot of photographs. Tabloids are usually considered to be less serious than other newspapers.

[2] If you **regale** people with songs or stories, you entertain them.

[3] The **patron saint** of a place, an activity, or a group of people is a saint who is believed to give them special help and protection.

[4] If something is **marred**, it is spoiled or damaged.

[5] **Hawking** something is selling it, usually on the street.

[6] An **elixir** is a liquid that is considered to have magical powers.

◄ A 107-year-old Calabrian man has helped produce olive oil throughout his life.

IN CALABRIA, THE HUNT for hidden molecules and **mechanisms** that confer longevity on people like Salvatore Caruso begins in places like the *Ufficio Anagrafe Stato Civile* (Civil Registry Office) in the medieval village of Luzzi. The office windows here offer stunning views of snow-covered mountains to the north, but to a population geneticist the truly breathtaking sights are hidden inside the tall file cabinets ringing the room and on shelf after shelf of precious ledgers numbered by year, starting in 1866. Despite its well-earned reputation for chaos and disorganization, the Italian government, shortly after the **unification** of the country in 1861, ordered local officials to record the birth, marriage, and death of every citizen in each *comune*, or township.

Since 1994, scientists at the University of Calabria have combed through these records in every one of Calabria's 409 *comuni* to compile an extraordinary survey. Coupling family histories with simple physiological[7] measurements of frailty

and the latest genomic technologies, they set out to address fundamental questions about longevity. How much of it is determined by genetics? How much by the environment? And how do these factors interact to promote longevity—or, **conversely,** to hasten the aging process? To answer all those questions, scientists must start with rock-solid demographic[8] data.

"Here is the book from 1905," explained Marco Giordano, one of Giuseppe Passarino's young colleagues, opening a tall green ledger. He pointed to a record, in careful cursive, of the birth of Francesco D'Amato on March 3, 1905. "He died in 2007," Giordano noted, describing D'Amato as the central figure of an extensive genealogical tree. "We can **reconstruct** the pedigrees[9] of families from these records."

[7] **Physiology** is the study of how bodies function.

[8] **Demographic** information is information about people in a particular society or age group.

[9] Someone's **pedigree** is his or her background or ancestors.

Cross-checking the ledger entries against meticulously detailed registry cards (pink for women, white for men) going back to the 19th century, Giordano, along with researchers Alberto Montesanto and Cinzia Martino, has reconstructed extensive family trees of 202 nonagenarians and centenarians in Calabria. The records document not only siblings of people who lived to 100 but also the spouses of siblings, which has allowed Passarino's group to do a kind of historical experiment on longevity. "We compared the ages of D'Amato's brothers and sisters to the ages of their spouses," Giordano explained. "So they had the same environment. They ate the same food. They used the same medicines. They came from the same culture. But they did not have the same genes." In a 2011 paper, the Calabrian researchers reported a surprising conclusion: Although the parents and siblings of people who lived to at least 90 also

lived longer than the general population, a finding in line with earlier research, the genetic factors involved seemed to benefit males more than females.

The Calabrian results on gender offer yet another hint that the genetic twists and turns that confer longevity may be unusually complex. Major European studies had previously reported that women are much likelier to live to 100, **outnumbering** male centenarians by a **ratio** of four or five to one, with the **implication** that some of the reasons are genetic. But by teasing out details from family trees, the Calabrian researchers discovered an intriguing paradox: The genetic component of longevity appears to be stronger in males—but women may take better advantage of external factors such as diet and medical care than men do.

Getting to 100 candles

Centenarians reach that milestone because they're healthier, by virtue of genetics, common sense, or luck. In people with an average life span, diseases of old age strike earlier and last longer.

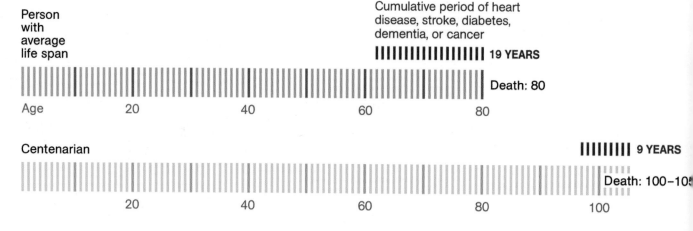

Person with average life span

Cumulative period of heart disease, stroke, diabetes, dementia, or cancer

||||||||||||||||||| 19 YEARS

|||||||||||||||||||||||||||||||||||||||||||||||||||||||||||||||||||||||||| Death: 80

Age   20   40   60   80

Centenarian

||||||||| 9 YEARS

|||||||||||||||||||||||||||||||||||||||||||||||||||||||||||||||||||||||||||||||||||||| Death: 100–105

20   40   60   80   100

NGM ART. SOURCE: THOMAS PERLS,
NEW ENGLAND CENTENARIAN STUDY, BOSTON UNIVERSITY

In the dimly lit, chilly hallway outside Passarino's university office stand several freezers full of tubes containing centenarian blood. The DNA from this blood and other tissue samples has revealed additional information about the Calabrian group. For example, people who live into their 90s and beyond tend to possess a particular version, or allele, of a gene important to taste and digestion. This allele not only gives people a taste for bitter foods like broccoli and field greens, which are typically rich in compounds known as polyphenols that promote cellular health, but also allows cells in the intestine to extract nutrients more efficiently from food as it's being digested.

Passarino has also found in his centenarians a revved-up[10] version of a gene for what is called an uncoupling protein. The protein plays a central role in metabolism—the way a person consumes energy and regulates body heat—which in turn affects the rate of aging.

"We have dissected five or six pathways that most influence longevity," says Passarino. "Most of them involve the response to stress, the metabolism of nutrients, or metabolism in general—the storage and use of energy." His group is currently examining how environmental influences—everything from childhood diet to how long a person attends school—might modify the activity of genes in a way that either promotes or curtails longevity.

[10] If something is **revved up**, it is more active than usual.

▼ A 96-year-old man uses his all-terrain vehicle to run errands on Ikaria Island, Greece.

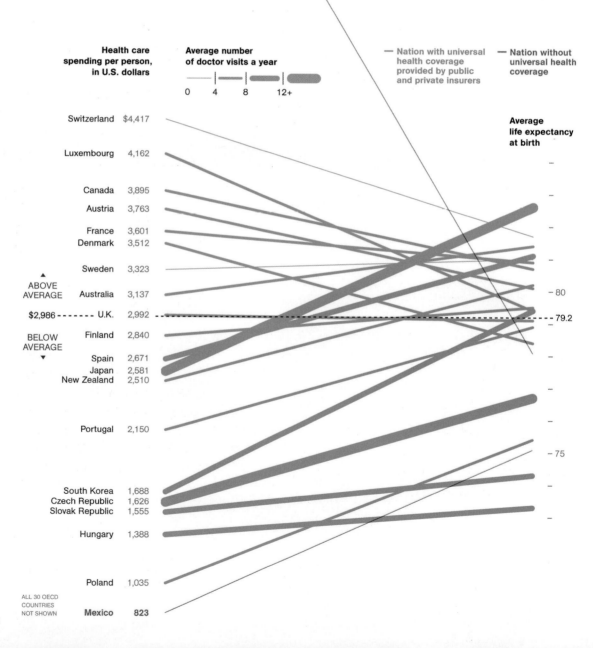

The Cost of Care

The United States spends more on medical care per person than any country, yet life expectancy is shorter than in most other developed nations and many developing ones. Lack of health insurance is a factor in life span and contributes to an estimated 45,000 deaths a year. Why the high cost? The U.S. has a fee-for-service system that pays medical providers piecemeal for appointments, surgery, and the like. That can lead to unneeded treatment that doesn't reliably improve a patient's health. Says Gerard Anderson, a professor at Johns Hopkins Bloomberg Schoo of Public Health who studies health insurance worldwide, "More care does not necessarily mean better care."

United States $7,290

Health care spending per person, in U.S. dollars

Average number of doctor visits a year

0   4   8   12+

— Nation with universal health coverage provided by public and private insurers

— Nation without universal health coverage

Average life expectancy at birth

Country	Spending
Switzerland	$4,417
Luxembourg	4,162
Canada	3,895
Austria	3,763
France	3,601
Denmark	3,512
Sweden	3,323
Australia	3,137
U.K.	2,992
Finland	2,840
Spain	2,671
Japan	2,581
New Zealand	2,510
Portugal	2,150
South Korea	1,688
Czech Republic	1,626
Slovak Republic	1,555
Hungary	1,388
Poland	1,035
Mexico	823

▲ ABOVE AVERAGE

$2,986 ------- U.K.

BELOW AVERAGE ▼

80

79.2

75

ALL 30 OECD COUNTRIES NOT SHOWN

Yoga exercise is believed to be one contributing factor to longevity.

AROUND THE WORLD, STUDIES are being done to determine the causes of longevity and health in old age. If nothing else, the plethora of new studies indicates that longevity researchers are pushing the scientific conversation to a new level. In October 2011, the Archon Genomics X Prize launched a race among research teams to sequence the DNA of a hundred centenarians (dubbing the contest "100 over 100").

But genes alone are unlikely to explain all the secrets of longevity, and experts see a cautionary tale[11] in recent results concerning caloric restriction. Experiments on 41 different genetic models of mice, for example, have shown that restricting food intake produces wildly **contradictory** outcomes. About half the mouse species lived longer, but just as many lived less time on a restricted diet than they would have on a normal diet. And last August, a long-running National Institute on Aging experiment on primates concluded that monkeys kept on a restricted-calorie

diet for 25 years showed no longevity advantage. Passarino made the point while driving back to his laboratory after visiting the centenarians in Molochio. "It's not that there are good genes and bad genes," he said. "It's certain genes at certain times. And in the end, genes probably account for only 25 percent of longevity. It's the environment, too, but that doesn't explain all of it either. And don't forget chance."

Which brought to mind Salvatore Caruso of Molochio, 107 years old and still going strong. Because he broke his leg 88 years ago, he was unfit to serve in the Italian Army when his entire unit was recalled during World War II. "They were all sent to the Russian front," he said, "and not a single one of them came back." It's another reminder that although molecules and mechanisms yet unfathomed[12] may someday lead to drugs that help us reach a ripe and healthy old age, a little luck doesn't hurt either.

[11] A **cautionary tale** is one that is intended to give a warning to people.

[12] If something is **unfathomed**, it is not understood or explained, usually because it is very strange or complicated.

A | Understanding Main Ideas. Write answers to the questions about the main ideas in "Beyond 100."

1. Why is Calabria a good place to study longevity?

   _____

   _____

2. What are some of the main points scientists have learned about longevity?

   _____

   _____

   _____

   _____

B | Identifying Key Details. Work with a partner. Find information in the reading passage to answer these questions.

1. Why did the researchers compare centenarians with their spouses and siblings?

   _____

   _____

2. What tools did the researchers use to make family trees of people in Calabria?

   _____

   _____

3. What are two ways that genetics can contribute to longevity?

   _____

   _____

4. What evidence shows that caloric restriction may not lead to longevity?

   _____

   _____

C | Identifying Supporting Examples. Complete the chart on the next page with information about how three factors affect the lives of each individual or group. If the information is not included in the reading, leave the space blank.

	Genetics	External Factors	Chance
Domenico Romeo			
Maria Rosa Caruso			
Salvatore Caruso			
Men, in general			
Women, in general			

D | Identifying Meaning from Context. Find and underline the following words in the reading passage on pages 171–177. Use context to help you match each word with its definition.

1. _____ Paragraph C: **prodigiously**   a. a state of complete disorder and confusion

2. _____ Paragraph C: **impish**   b. largely, impressively

3. _____ Paragraph G: **undermined**   c. disrespectful or naughty in a playful way

4. _____ Paragraph H: **dubious**   d. not completely honest, safe, or reliable

5. _____ Paragraph I: **breathtaking**   e. made something less strong or less secure

6. _____ Paragraph I: **chaos**   f. very carefully and with great attention to detail

7. _____ Paragraph L: **meticulously**   g. extremely beautiful or amazing

8. _____ Paragraph L: **nonagenarians**   h. a situation that involves two things that seem to contradict each other

9. _____ Paragraph M: **paradox**   i. people who are between 90 and 99 years old

E | Identifying Meaning from Context. Find and underline the following phrases on pages 171–177. Use the context to help you match each phrase with the best meaning. (Some of these phrases have similar meanings.)

1. _____ Paragraph G: **fallen on hard times**
2. _____ Paragraph H: **turning up**
3. _____ Paragraph J: **combed through**
4. _____ Paragraph M: **teasing out**
5. _____ Paragraph S: **brought to mind**

    a. looked very carefully at information in order to find something

    b. begun a difficult period

    c. made someone think of something

    d. successfully uncovering something that is difficult to get

    e. separating out particular facts from a great deal of information

F | Understanding Infographics. Write answers to the questions about the infographic on page 176.

1. Which country spends the most per person on health care? The least?

    Most: _____ Least: _____

2. Which countries have the highest number of annual doctor visits? The lowest?

    Highest: _____

    Lowest: _____

3. Which country has the longest life expectancy? The shortest?

    Longest: _____ Shortest: _____

G | Critical Thinking: Making Inferences. Based on the infographic on page 176, what inferences can be made about the relationship between health care spending and longevity? What can be inferred about the relationship between doctor visits and longevity?

_____

_____

_____

H | Personalizing. Write an answer to the following question and share your answer with a partner.

Would you like to live to be a centenarian? Why, or why not?

_____

_____

_____

Before Viewing

A | **Using a Dictionary.** Here are some words you will hear in the video. Match each one with the correct definition. Use your dictionary to help you.

1. _____: sitting down a lot of the time and not doing much exercise

2. _____: having deep religious beliefs

3. _____: the state of being extremely overweight

4. _____: disconnect yourself from all forms of technology for a period of time

> devout
> obesity
> sedentary
> unplug

 B | **Thinking Ahead.** What are some habits that can help people live longer? Make a list with a partner.

While Viewing

A | Watch the video about longevity. As you watch, check your answers to exercise **B** in "Before Viewing." Circle the topics that are mentioned in the video.

B | Read questions 1–4. Think about the answers as you view the video.

1. What habits do the people of Sardinia, Okinawa, and Loma Linda have in common?
2. How is the reason for longevity in Loma Linda different from the reason for longevity in Sardinia and Okinawa?
3. In which places is the culture of longevity disappearing? Why?
4. The culture of longevity is not disappearing in one of the places. Why?

After Viewing

 A | Discuss your answers to questions (1–4) above with a partner.

 B | **Critical Thinking: Synthesizing.** Discuss your answers to the questions (1–3) in a small group.

1. The narrator of the video is surprised that both men and women in Sardinia live long lives. How might Giuseppe Passarino and Maurizio Berardelli (from the reading on pages 171–177) explain this phenomenon?
2. The narrator states that people in Okinawa may live longer because they practice caloric restriction. How might Passarino and Berardelli respond to this statement?
3. Which is more recent, the video or the article? How do you know?

GOAL: Writing an Argumentative Research Paper

In this lesson, you are going to plan, write, revise, and edit a research paper on the following topic: *Should scientists spend time, money, and resources to help people live 100 years or longer?*

Writing Skills: Planning a Research Paper

In an essay, the writer usually presents his or her own views about a topic and may or may not refer to sources. A research paper is different because it must include information from outside sources, such as journals, books, and websites.

An argumentative research paper involves expressing an opinion on a topic and then using researched examples and evidence to support the thesis. There are several steps involved in planning an argumentative research paper.

Choose a topic: Pick something that you can research and that you can argue about. (In this unit, the topic is chosen for you.) Consider a possible thesis statement or question, but be flexible. You may change your mind after you do some research.

Brainstorm ideas: Make a T-chart to brainstorm ideas that answer your question or ideas that support your possible argument and the opposite argument.

Do research: Take notes on relevant information that supports your potential thesis. Use index cards so it's easy to organize your notes later. Your teacher may specify a minimum number of sources. (Review Researching and Note-taking in Unit 7, page 159).

Draft a thesis statement: Decide what your overall argument, or thesis statement, will be.

Make an outline: Ask: *What is the best way to convince my readers that my argument is valid? What idea do I want to share first? What do I want to share next? What evidence supports each idea?* Draft a basic outline of your paper and organize your note cards to follow your outline. Then complete your outline with information from your note cards.

A | Critical Thinking: Evaluating. Check (✓) the statements that are possible argumentative research topics.

☐ 1. Cigarette advertisements are no longer permitted in some countries.

☐ 2. Alcohol advertisements on television are harmful.

☐ 3. There would be fewer auto accidents if the legal driving age were changed to 21.

☐ 4. The legal driving age is different all over the world.

☐ 5. Cigarette smoking around children should be made illegal.

☐ 6. In the past, tobacco was used medicinally.

B | Critical Thinking: Evaluating. Check (✓) the four pieces of evidence that best support the following thesis: "Cigarette smoking around children should be made illegal."

☐ 1. A lot of people smoke cigarettes around their children.

☐ 2. Some cigarette advertisements target children.

☐ 3. According to James Garbarino of Cornell University, "More young children are killed by parental smoking than by all unintentional injuries combined."

☐ 4. A recent study shows that the children of smokers are more likely to become smokers than children whose parents don't smoke.

☐ 5. A recent German study showed that teenagers who are exposed to tobacco ads are more likely to start smoking than teens who don't see these ads.

☐ 6. World Health Organization statistics show that tobacco use kills six million people a year.

☐ 7. According to the World Health Organization, 600,000 nonsmokers die from secondhand smoke every year.

C | Brainstorming. Consider the following question: *Should scientists spend time, money, and resources so that people can live 100 years or longer? Or would the money be better spent elsewhere?* Explore the question by completing the T-chart with your own ideas.

Yes, scientists should spend time, money, and resources for this.	No, scientists should not spend time, money, and resources for this.
This research may help us all be healthier.	If most people live to 100, who will take care of all the elderly people?

D | Researching and Note-taking. Research the topic and take notes. Decide on your thesis statement and add ideas to your T-chart in exercise **C**.

Language for Writing: Explaining the Significance of Evidence

Evidence doesn't stand on its own. In other words, as a writer, you have to show your readers why a piece of evidence is important. After you have provided a piece of evidence from your research, explain how that evidence supports your argument. You can introduce your explanation with the following phrases:

This research shows that . . .   This supports the idea that . . .

As this evidence shows, . . .   This demonstrates . . .

For example: *A recent German study showed that teenagers who are exposed to tobacco ads are more likely to start smoking than teens who don't see these ads.* **This research shows that** *tobacco advertisements negatively affect teenagers, encouraging them to start smoking and potentially increasing their chances of having tobacco-related medical problems such as lung cancer and stroke.*

E | Applying. Write an explanation for each piece of evidence that supports the following thesis statement: "Cigarette smoking around children should be made illegal."

1. According to James Garbarino of Cornell University, "More young children are killed by parental smoking than by all unintentional injuries combined."

   _____

   _____

   _____

2. According to the World Health Organization, 600,000 nonsmokers die from secondhand smoke every year.

   _____

   _____

   _____

3. World Health Organization statistics show that tobacco use kills six million people a year.

   _____

   _____

   _____

4. A recent study shows that the children of smokers are more likely to become smokers than children whose parents don't smoke.

   _____

   _____

   _____

A | **Planning.** Follow the steps to make an outline for your research paper.

Step 1   Write notes about the background of your topic. For example, what are scientists doing? Why are they doing it?

Step 2   Write your thesis statement from exercise **D** on page 184 in the outline.

Step 3   Choose three arguments from your T-chart on page 183 to support your thesis. It is often a good idea to present your strongest argument last.

Step 4   Write a topic sentence for each of your body paragraphs. Remember to reflect your key concepts in your topic sentences.

Step 5   For each body paragraph, write one or two pieces of evidence that support the ideas in your topic sentences. Include reasons why the evidence is significant.

Step 6   Write ideas for your conclusion.

Introductory paragraph:

Give some background about the topic (e.g., what scientists are currently doing to gather information about longevity). What is your thesis statement?

_____

_____

1st body paragraph: What is one argument in support of your thesis?

Topic sentence: _____

Explanation and examples: _____

_____

_____

2nd body paragraph: What is a second argument in support of your thesis?

Topic sentence: _____

Explanation and examples: _____

_____

_____

3rd body paragraph: What is the strongest argument in support of your thesis?

Topic sentence: _____

Explanation and examples: _____

_____

_____

Concluding paragraph: Review your main points and your thesis statement.

_____

_____

B | **Draft 1.** Use your outline to write a first draft of your paper.

One way to cite your sources is to include the last name of the author and the year in parentheses. If you introduce your information with the author's name, you include only the year in parentheses. This paper uses the APA (American Psychological Association) style.

In the 1500s, when Europeans began using tobacco, people were not aware of the dangers of smoking. In fact, according to the article "Tobacco: From Miracle Cure to Toxin," doctors often prescribed tobacco as medicine, believing it could cure cancer and many other diseases (Wexler, 2006). But in the early 20th century, people began to suspect that tobacco was dangerous rather than helpful. These days, it is widely accepted that cigarette smoking is dangerous and can cause medical problems such as lung cancer and stroke. In some countries, tobacco companies are required to include health warnings on their cigarette packs. Right now, many people believe that secondhand smoke is dangerous, but not everyone agrees. Therefore, there are no laws protecting nonsmokers from secondhand smoke. As history has shown, we have been wrong about the safety of tobacco in the past and people suffered as a result. For that reason, new laws should be created that make it illegal to smoke around children.

You can use the backgrou information in opening para to lead your r to your thesis statement.

Research shows that secondhand smoke endangers nonsmokers' lives. The World Health Organization (WHO) states that 600,000 nonsmokers die from secondhand smoke every year. Approximately 28 percent of these people are children. According to the WHO's statistics, 40 percent of children have at least one smoking parent (2013). It's true that secondhand smoke is everywhere, and making smoking illegal around children won't protect them from all secondhand smoke. Nevertheless, as James Garbarino of Cornell University states, "More young children are killed by parental smoking than by all unintentional injuries combined" (Lang, 1998). If children were not forced to breathe their parents' secondhand smoke, their exposure to tobacco smoke would decrease dramatically. This demonstrates that enacting laws that prohibit people from smoking around children would have a positive impact on children's health and life expectancy.

You can introduce opposing argumen in your research pa and then refute the

Of course, secondhand smoke endangers everyone, not just children. However, laws should be enacted to protect children specifically because they can't protect themselves. If an adult doesn't want to be around secondhand smoke, he or she can just walk away. However, children don't always have that option. Children of smokers are especially in danger of suffering from secondhand smoke because smoking occurs in their homes every day. Secondhand smoke might be in every breath that they breathe. In addition, secondhand smoke affects infants differently than it does adults. According to WHO, while secondhand smoke can cause serious heart and lung diseases in adults, it can cause sudden death in infants (2013).

In addition to endangering children's health, exposure to smoking encourages children to smoke as teenagers and adults. According to an article in *Medical News Today*, a study showed that the children of smokers were "more than two times as likely to begin smoking cigarettes on a daily basis between the ages of 13 and 21 than were children whose parents didn't use tobacco" (Schwarz, 2005). This greatly increases the child's chances of an early death. WHO statistics show that tobacco use kills six million people a year (2013). These statistics combined show that exposure to smoking is deadly for children, and lives would be saved if smoking around children were illegal.

Cigarette smoking is so popular that it will probably never completely disappear, even though people are aware of the dangers. However, there are things we can do in order to protect nonsmokers, especially children. Making it illegal to smoke around children would result in fewer children dying from secondhand smoke and fewer children becoming smokers. Perhaps most importantly, it would protect those who can't protect themselves.

Reference List

Lang, Susan S. (1998, Spring). Child protection expert says parental smoking is abuse. Human Ecology Forum, 26, 22. Retrieved from http://www.redwoods.edu/instruct/jjohnston/English1A/readings/smoking/smokingisabuse.htm

Schwarz, Joel. (2005, September 28). Children whose parents smoked are twice as likely to begin smoking between ages 13 and 21 as offspring of nonsmokers. University of Washington. Retrieved from http://www.washington.edu/news/2005/09/28/children-whose-parents-smoked-are-twice-as-likely-to-begin-smoking-between-ages-13-and-21-as-offspring-of-nonsmokers/

Wexler, Thomas A. (2006, June 12). Tobacco: from miracle cure to toxin. YaleGlobal Online. Retrieved from yaleglobal.yale.edu/about/tobacco.jsp

World Health Organization. (2013, July). Tobacco: fact sheet N° 339. Retreived from www.who.int/mediacentre/factsheets/fs339/en/

Step 1   Underline the thesis statement.

Step 2   Check (✓) the sentences that provide opposing viewpoints.

Step 3   Underline the topic sentences of the body paragraphs.

Step 4   Circle each piece of evidence in the body paragraphs.

Step 5   Underline the main points that are reviewed in the conclusion.

D | **Revising.** Complete steps 1–5 in exercise **C** on your own research paper.

E | **Peer Evaluation.** Exchange your first draft with a partner and follow these steps.

Step 1   Read your partner's research paper and tell him or her one thing that you liked about it.

Step 2   Complete the outline showing the ideas that your partner's research paper describes.

Introductory paragraph:

Give some background about the topic (e.g., what scientists are currently doing to gather information about longevity). What is your thesis statement?

_____

_____

1st body paragraph: What is one argument in support of your thesis?

Topic sentence: _____

Explanation and examples: _____

_____

_____

2nd body paragraph: What is a second argument in support of your thesis?

Topic sentence: _____

Explanation and examples: _____

_____

_____

3rd body paragraph: What is the strongest argument in support of your thesis?

Topic sentence: _____

Explanation and examples: _____

_____

_____

Concluding paragraph: Review your main points and your thesis statement.

_____

_____

Step 3 Compare this outline with the one that your partner created in exercise **A** on page 185.

Step 4 The two outlines should be similar. If they aren't, discuss how they differ.

F | Draft 2. Write a second draft of your paper. Use what you learned from the peer evaluation activity and your answers to exercise **D**. Make any other necessary changes.

G | Editing Checklist. Use the checklist to find errors in your second draft.

Editing Checklist	Yes	No
1. Are all the words spelled correctly?		
2. Does every sentence have correct punctuation?		
3. Do your subjects and verbs agree?		
4. Are your verb tenses correct?		
5. Have you used explanation phrases correctly?		

H | Final Draft. Now use your Editing Checklist to write a third draft of your research paper. Make any necessary changes.

Memorable Experiences

ACADEMIC PATHWAYS
Lesson A: Making inferences
                Analyzing a personal narrative
Lesson B: Using sensory details
                Writing an extended personal narrative

◄ Hitchhiking
travelers signal for
a lift to Moscow on
the Russian Steppe.

Think and Discuss

1. What is your most memorable travel experience? What made it memorable?
2. In what ways can travel teach us important lessons about life?

Exploring the Theme

Great thinkers and writers have been describing the value of travel for centuries. Read some of their thoughts on travel, meeting people, and gaining new experiences. Then discuss them using the following questions.

1. What does each quotation mean? Explain it in your own words.
2. Which quotation do you most agree with? Are there any that you disagree with? Explain your answers.
3. Do you know any quotations that are similar to these in your native language? If so, share them with your classmates.

For many people, traveling is more than just moving from one place to another. Travel can be a kind of education, one that is acquired through experiences— experiences with new and unfamiliar people, places, and customs. How we deal with these experiences and what we learn from them can often have more value than an education at one of the world's greatest universities.

There are no foreign lands. It is the traveler only who is foreign.

Robert Louis Stevenson, American writer

There are no strangers here; Only friends you haven't yet met.

William Butler Yeats, British poet

Travelers climb the immense sand ▲ dunes in the Sossuvlei region of Namibia's Namib-Naukluft Park.

Traveling—it leaves you speechless, then turns you into a storyteller.

Ibn Battuta, Moroccan and Berber explorer

No one realizes how beautiful it is to travel until he comes home and rests his head on his old, familiar pillow.

Lin Yutang, Chinese writer

WE LIVE IN A WONDERFUL WORLD THAT IS FULL OF BEAUTY, CHARM AND ADVENTURE. THERE IS NO END TO THE ADVENTURES WE CAN HAVE IF ONLY WE SEEK THEM WITH OUR EYES OPEN.

Jawaharlal Nehru, Indian prime minister

To awaken quite alone in a strange town is one of the pleasantest sensations in the world.

Freya Stark, British explorer

Perhaps travel . . . by demonstrating that all peoples cry, laugh, eat, worry, and die, can introduce the idea that if we try and understand each other, we may even become friends.

Maya Angelou, American poet

A traveler without observation is a bird without wings.

Moslih Eddin Saadi, Persian poet

A | **Building Vocabulary.** Use the context to guess the meanings of the words in **blue**. Then write the words next to their definitions (1–7).

Why do we remember some events more clearly than others? Studies show that being in a heightened emotional state when an event occurs may **ensure** better retention of the event. One type of emotional memory is a flashbulb memory. A flashbulb memory often happens when people are **confronted** with a shocking event. For example, years after the September 11, 2001 attacks, many people can remember exactly what they were doing when they heard about them.

As strange as it may seem, when I remember the **massive** 7.1 earthquake that occurred in San Francisco in 1989, I have very positive feelings. I was only six years old at the time, and I recall not being the least bit afraid. Because the electricity was off, I didn't see any frightening images on TV. My parents were calm and positive. The neighbors all got together to share their food so it wouldn't spoil. It was like one big party. When I went back to school, though, I realized that other kids were very traumatized by the event. I think this taught me a valuable lesson: Your own experience with reality often **transcends** what other people tell you about it.

Should parents take their children out of class to go on trips during the school year? Many U.S. elementary schools don't think so. However, a recent study shows that children benefit when they are **exposed** to new cultures and experiences through travel. A recent survey showed that school-aged children who took time off from class for travel had higher grade point averages and were more likely to attend college than other children. Although in most cases schools do not give children time off for travel, some schools will allow it if students complete school **assignments** while on the road. In addition, many parents **devise** assignments for their children such as keeping a journal or photo log, which have the added benefit of creating lasting memories.

1. _____: introduced to an experience

2. _____: goes beyond normal limits or boundaries

3. _____: challenged by or forced to deal with something

4. _____: tasks or work that people have to do, usually of an academic nature

5. _____: to have an idea for something and design it

6. _____: very large

7. _____: make certain that something happens

B | Building Vocabulary. Complete the definitions (1–5) with the words from the box.

> compelled   conceived   desperate   intervene   assumptions

1. If you make _____ about someone, you form an opinion about him or her without any real proof.

2. If you are _____, you are in such a bad situation that you are willing to try anything to change it.

3. If you _____ in a situation, you become involved in it and try to change it.

4. If you feel _____ to do something, you feel that you must do it because it is the right thing to do.

5. If a plan has been _____, it has been thought of.

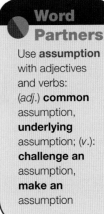

Word Partners
Use **assumption** with adjectives and verbs:
(*adj.*) **common** assumption, **underlying** assumption; (*v.*): **challenge an** assumption, **make an** assumption

C | Using Vocabulary. Answer the questions. Share your ideas with a partner.

1. Have you ever felt **compelled** to make a big change in your life? Explain your answer.

2. If you saw two people fighting on the street, would you **intervene**? Why, or why not?

3. Can you think of a time when you **made assumptions about** people that were not correct? Explain your answer.

D | Brainstorming. Can you think of examples when your first impressions of a place turned out to be wrong? Share your ideas in a small group.

_____

_____

_____

E | Predicting. Read paragraphs A and B on page 195. What do you think will happen next in the story? Note your ideas below. Then check your predictions as you read the rest of the passage.

_____

_____

_____

Welcome Stranger

by Sebastian Junger

▲ A lone truck travels down a dirt track
near the town of Gillette, Wyoming, USA.

> Author Sebastian
> Junger learns that first
> impressions are often
> wrong—and other hard-
> won lessons from the road.

track **2-04**

A

MY PLAN WAS TO CROSS MONTANA, Idaho, and Washington before it got too cold, then work my way down to Los Angeles and return home across the desert and the Deep South. I figured I'd make it back by Christmas. My first night was spent in a blizzard in the South Dakota Badlands, the second in the desolate little town of Gillette, Wyoming. The next morning, I limped out to the highway and stood in the shrieking wind under a high, cold, cloudless sky with my thumb jabbed out. Freight liners barreled[1] past me. Locals drove by in pickups and threw beer bottles that exploded against the frozen pavement.

B

After two or three hours, I saw a man working his way toward me along the on-ramp from town. He wore filthy canvas coveralls and carried a black lunch box, and as he got closer, I could see that his hair was matted in a way that occurs only after months on the skids. Gillette was a hard-bitten mining town that had fallen on bad times, and I thought that anyone walking out to the highway looking like that on a 20-degree (minus 6-degree Celsius) day was probably pretty **desperate**. I put my hand on the pepper spray[2] in my pocket and turned to face him. My backpack was on the pavement by my feet. I was ready.

C

"You been out here long?" he asked.

I nodded.

"Where you headed?"

"California."

"Warm out there."

"Yup."

"You got enough food?"

D

I thought about this. Clearly, he didn't have any, and if I admitted that I did, he'd ask for some. That in itself wasn't a problem, but it would mean opening my backpack and revealing all my obviously expensive camping gear. I felt alone and **exposed** and ripe for pillage,[3] and I just didn't want to do that. Twenty years later, I still remember my answer: "I got some cheese."

[1] If a vehicle or a person is **barreling**, it is moving very quickly.
[2] **Pepper spray** is a chemical compound in an aerosol that is used as a self-defense weapon.
[3] **Pillage** is stealing other people's property using violent methods. If someone is **ripe for pillage**, he or she is in a situation in which it is likely that another person will take something from him or her.

E   "You won't make it to California with just a little cheese," he said. "You'll starve." At first, I didn't understand. What was he saying, exactly? I kept my hand on the pepper spray.

F   "Believe me," he said, "I know. Listen, I'm living in a car back in town, and every day I walk out to the mine to see if they need me. Today they don't, so I won't be needing this lunch of mine."

G   I began to sag with understanding. In his world, whatever you have in your bag is all you've got, and he knew "a little cheese" would never get me to California.

H   "I'm fine, really," I said. "I don't need your lunch."

I   He shook his head and opened his box. It was a typical church meal—a bologna sandwich, an apple, and a bag of chips—and I kept protesting, but he wouldn't hear of it. I finally took his lunch and watched him walk back down the on-ramp toward town. I learned a lot of things in college, I thought, and I learned a lot from the books I'd read on my own. I had learned things in Newfoundland and in Europe and in Mexico and in my hometown of Belmont, Massachusetts, but I had to stand out there on that frozen piece of interstate to learn true generosity from a homeless man.

J   The lessons were piling up.[4] You had to be wary when you traveled, I realized, but you also had to be open. You had to protect yourself, but you couldn't be so suspicious that you'd lie to avoid giving food to a stranger. These were lessons from the harsher parts of the world, but I started to think that maybe they were applicable anywhere. It seemed as though there must be a way of traveling that made you ready for anything. The starting point was respect; if you didn't lead with that, even with street-corner thugs,[5] nothing was going to turn out well. So you start with respect and see where it goes; if it doesn't work, you switch to something else. On a highway on-ramp in Wyoming, everyone is equal, more or less. No one has a past, no one has a future, and things pretty much come down to how you treat one another. There's a certain liberty in that; there's a certain justice.

[4] If things are **piling up**, they are increasing in number.
[5] **Thugs** are violent people or criminals.

A snowy path ▶ leads toward the Sierra de Gredos mountains, Spain.

Obviously, the more money you spend when you're traveling, the less likely you are to find yourself in those situations. And yet. I once said "sir" to a doorman at a fancy hotel, and a friend asked me why I'd done that. I can't remember my answer exactly, but I suspect that it related to that guy out on the highway. He's always with me, in a way, reminding me not to **make assumptions about** people, reminding me to keep my heart open. Everyone has a role in the world, and who is to say which role is more worthy or admirable than any other.

That became a cornerstone[6] of my journalism. Since every person I've interviewed has led a life unique to them, they have something to say about the world that I couldn't get from anyone else. That gives them a value that **transcends** any job or social rank they might have. I began to see that you could divide up the world in many different ways, and some of those ways actually put a homeless man from Wyoming at the top. He might not have known it, but I do, and the point of much of my work has been to communicate that.

I kept traveling, and I kept learning. Once, I caught a bus up into a wild and remote part of western Spain called the Sierra de Gredos because I'd heard there were still wolves up there . It was a hasty plan **conceived** the night before in a barroom in Salamanca, and as soon as I stepped off the bus, I realized that I was in over my head: It was snowing hard, and the mountain town where I found myself seemed completely deserted. There wasn't even a hotel. In the quickly gathering dusk, I started walking back down the road looking for a place to spend the night. The only plan I could **devise** was to build a fire and try to keep myself awake until dawn, but after five or ten minutes of walking, I saw a lone pair of headlights coming down the mountainside. The car made its way slowly along the switchbacks,[7] and when it approached me, the driver stopped and rolled down the window. "Get in," he said. "No one walks in these mountains at night. You'll die."

[6] The **cornerstone** of something is the basic part of it on which its existence, success, or truth depends.

[7] A **switchback** is a road that goes up a steep hill in a series of sharp bends.

An hour later, I was back in that bar in Salamanca. What sense of responsibility, I wondered, had **compelled** that man to stop? He had no idea whether or not I was dangerous, and yet he took a risk to **ensure** that a complete stranger would be OK. It seemed as though he understood there to be some sort of general citizenship in the world, and that if a fellow citizen were threatened, it was his duty—everyone's duty—to **intervene**.

As I got older, I traveled less for its own sake and more for journalism **assignments**. I found myself covering wars in West Africa and Afghanistan and the Balkans—situations that were far more dangerous than the aimless trips of my youth. However, those early trips undoubtedly affected me more than I'd realized at the time. They may not have taught me the specific skills of my new trade, but it was in places like Spain and Mexico where I first learned how to comport myself [8] in the world.

Many years later, I **confronted** the daunting task of walking into a fishermen's bar in Gloucester, Massachusetts, and asking the bartender—a woman named Ethel Shatford—about the death of her son. A local boat, the *Andrea Gail*, had gone down in a **massive** storm in 1991, and the book I wrote about her was eventually published as *The Perfect Storm*. The Crow's Nest was the sort of bar where everyone turns to look at a stranger as soon as he walks in. I ignored the stares, took a seat at the bar, and ordered a beer from Ethel.

[8] If you **comport yourself** in a particular way, you behave that way.

I had no idea how to begin, but I had help. They were all still with me, I realized—the man in Wyoming and the rest of the people I've met on my travels—they were still there, guiding and informing me, whispering their lessons in my ear. And in one way or another, they all had something to tell me about how I should approach Ethel Shatford.

Just tell her, I finally thought. Tell her she knows something about the world that a lot of other people might need to hear.

◄ A monument in Gloucester, Massachusetts honors the memory of fishermen who died at sea.

THEY THAT GO DOWN TO THE SEA IN SHIPS
1623 — 1923

A | **Identifying Purpose.** Write answers to the questions. Share your ideas with a partner.

1. What do you know about the writer of "Welcome Stranger"?

   _____

   _____

2. What was the writer's purpose? Why did he name the article "Welcome Stranger"?

   _____

   _____

3. What do you think is the overall message of the article?

   _____

   _____

B | **Identifying Purpose and Structure.** What is the purpose of each of the main parts of "Welcome Stranger"? Match each part of the reading with its purpose.

a. A–I   1. _____ to show how past lessons helped the writer accomplish a difficult task in the present

b. J–L

c. M–N   2. _____ to describe a second travel experience and the lesson it contained

d. O

e. P–R   3. _____ to connect the past with the present

                  4. _____ to describe an experience of meeting someone while traveling

                  5. _____ to reflect on the meaning of a travel experience and others like it

C | **Identifying Key Details.** Answer the questions about "Welcome Stranger." Note the paragraphs in which you find the answers.

1. What was Junger's first impression of the man he sees on the on-ramp? Paragraph: _____

   _____

   _____

2. How did Junger interpret the homeless man's questions? Paragraph: _____

   _____

   _____

3. Why was Junger surprised by the homeless man? Paragraph: _____

_____

_____

4. What are Junger's "rules" for traveling? What is the most important rule, according to Junger?
Paragraph: _____

_____

_____

5. What does the incident with the doorman illustrate? Paragraph: _____

_____

_____

6. What became the cornerstone of Junger's journalism? How has it helped him in his work?
Paragraph: _____

_____

_____

7. What situation taught Junger that some people will take a risk to help others?
Paragraph: _____

_____

_____

8. How did Junger's lessons help him interview Ethel Shatford? Paragraph: _____

_____

_____

D | Identifying Meaning from Context. Find and underline the following phrases in the reading passage on pages 194–198. Use context to help you match each phrase with its definition.

1. _____ Paragraph A: **work my way (down to)**   a. not make assumptions

2. _____ Paragraph B: **on the skids**   b. use as a starting point

3. _____ Paragraph J: **lead with (something)**   c. confronting a situation that I'm not prepared for

4. _____ Paragraph K: **keep my heart open**   d. seemingly difficult or frightening job

5. _____ Paragraph M: **in over my head**   e. in a bad situation, especially economically

6. _____ Paragraph P: **daunting task**   f. travel toward

E | Critical Thinking: Making Inferences. Work with a partner. Use clues in "Welcome Stranger" to make inferences about Junger. Underline any words in the story that help you answer the questions (1–5).

1. Why does Junger initially refuse the homeless man's lunch?

   _____

   _____

2. Why do you think Junger was hitchhiking across the United States instead of driving or taking some other form of transportation?

   _____

   _____

3. How old do you think Junger is at the time the story takes place?

   _____

   _____

4. Why do you think Junger was carrying pepper spray?

   _____

   _____

5. What kind of person is Junger? What are some adjectives you might use to describe him?

   _____

   _____

F | Critical Thinking: Personalizing. Discuss the questions with a partner.

Have you ever been in any situations like the ones Junger describes in "Welcome Stranger"? If so, how were your experiences similar to his? If not, would you like to go on trips like the ones he describes? Why, or why not?

Reading Skill: Analyzing a Personal Narrative

When you analyze a narrative, you think about the following components:

- the **setting**: where the narrative takes place
- the **theme**: the main idea or the purpose of the narrative. For example, the theme of a story might be that hard work pays off or that you can't run away from your problems.
- the **mood**: the feeling the narrative communicates. Writers often communicate mood through word choice. For example, a writer can convey a positive mood by describing people or events as *delightful* or *joyful*.
- the **characters**: who the narrative is about
- the **plot**: the events, or anecdotes, that form the narrative's storyline

A | Analyzing. Discuss these questions about "Welcome Stranger" with a partner.

1. **Setting**: Where (in what places) does the narrative take place?

2. **Theme**: What is the theme of "Welcome Stranger"? In other words, what is the main idea of the story?

3. **Mood**: What is the mood of the narrative? What feelings does Junger communicate? What words help to convey the mood?

4. **Characters**: Who are the most important characters in the narrative? How would you describe the following characters?
   - Junger (narrator)
   - the homeless man

B | Retelling an Anecdote. There are two main anecdotes—short stories that illustrate an idea—in the story of "Welcome Stranger": the one with the homeless man and the one that takes place in Spain. Choose one and note the main events on the time line. Explain to a partner what happens first, second, third, and so on.

FRONTLINE DIARY

▲ The rugged terrain of Afghanistan provides the backdrop for this photograph by photojournalist Reza, taken from a helicopter gunship. In 2000, Reza accompanied Sebastian Junger on a visit to a region controlled by Ahmad Shah Massoud (1953–2001), an Afghan military leader who was fighting against the Taliban.

Before Viewing

A | Using a Dictionary. Here are some words and phrases you will hear in the video. Match each one with the correct definition. Use a dictionary to help you.

1. _____: take someone or something into a place secretly

2. _____: difficult or impossible to get to

3. _____: not understood or known about

4. _____: a state of disorder and confusion

> chaos
> inaccessible
> shrouded in mystery
> smuggle

 **B | Thinking Ahead.** What do you know about Afghanistan today? What do you know about its history? Share your ideas in a small group.

While Viewing

Read questions 1–4. Think about the answers as you view the video.

1. How does the narrator describe Afghanistan?

2. How do Junger and Reza get into the country? What makes the trip into Afghanistan dangerous?

3. On the first day at Massoud's headquarters, how does Junger describe breakfast?

4. In the feast scene at the end, how does Junger describe the Afghan people?

After Viewing

A | Discuss your answers to questions 1–4 above with a partner.

B | Critical Thinking: Synthesizing. What assumptions do you think Junger had about Afghanistan before his visit? How do you think his feelings changed? How does this experience compare with those he recounts in "Welcome Stranger"?

GOAL: Writing an Extended Personal Narrative

In this lesson, you are going to plan, write, revise, and edit an essay on the following topic: ***Describe a past experience that taught you a valuable life lesson.***

A | **Brainstorming.** Think of some lessons you have learned in life that you can connect with past experiences. Describe the experiences to your partner. Then discuss your answers to the questions.

1. Which experience is the most interesting?
2. Which one do you remember the best?
3. Which one do you remember the most details about?

B | **Vocabulary for Writing.** The following time words and phrases can be useful when writing a narrative. They help you show the order in which events occur. Write five sentences about the experiences you discussed in exercise **A** using these words and phrases.

after	after that	at first	before	during
eventually	finally	from . . . to . . .	later	meanwhile
next	the next time	now	one day	then
until	when	whenever	while	

_____

_____

_____

_____

_____

Free Writing. Write for five minutes. Describe one of the life lessons that you discussed in exercise **A**. Why was it an important lesson?

C | Read the information in the box. Then write sentences (1–4) using the cues with the simple past, the past perfect, and the past continuous. Sometimes more than one answer is possible.

Language for Writing: Reviewing Past Forms

When you write a narrative, you often use a variety of past verb forms. Use the simple past to describe events that were completed in the past.

> *Freight liners <u>barreled</u> past me.*

Combine the past continuous with the simple past to describe progressive events that occurred at the same time as completed past events, or that were interrupted by past events.

> *It <u>was snowing</u> hard and the mountain town where I <u>found</u> myself <u>seemed</u> completely deserted.*

> *I <u>was walking</u> along the ramp when a man <u>stopped</u> his car and <u>offered</u> me a ride.*

Use the past perfect to describe events that were completed in the past prior to other past events.

> *Gillette <u>was</u> a hard-bitten mining town that <u>had fallen</u> on bad times.*
>
>   **second event**   **first event**

Example

event in progress: we / drive in the desert

interrupting event: we / see an old man by the road

(when) _We were driving in the desert when we saw an old man by the road._

Or: _When we were driving in the desert, we saw an old man by the road._

1. event in progress: I / hike up a dusty trail

   interrupting event: I / encounter a rattlesnake

   (when) _____

2. first event: Belmont / become a busy working-class town

   second event: I / be born

   (by the time) _____

3. first: I / not really know the importance of trust

   second: I / started to spend a lot of time traveling

   (until) _____

4. first: we / go on vacation to Wyoming three times

   second: we / moved there last year

   (before) _____

Writing Skill: Using Sensory Details

Sensory details are details that show how things look, feel, smell, taste, or sound. Sensory details can enrich your writing style. They make sentences in narrative and descriptive writing more interesting because they help the reader experience what the writer is describing.

The next morning, I <u>limped</u> out to the highway and stood in the <u>shrieking</u> wind under a <u>high, cold, cloudless</u> sky with my thumb <u>jabbed</u> out.

Words like *limped* and *jabbed* convey body movements; they help you see how the narrator moved. *Shrieking* conveys how loud the wind sounded. *High, cold,* and *cloudless* paint a picture of how the sky looked.

D | **Critical Thinking: Analyzing.** Discuss in a small group the underlined sensory details in the sentences (1–6) from "Welcome Stranger." What do they convey? How do they help you more clearly understand what Junger is describing?

1. My first night was spent in a blizzard in the South Dakota Badlands, the second in the <u>desolate</u> little town of Gillette, Wyoming.

2. Freight liners <u>barreled</u> past me.

3. Locals drove by in pickups and threw beer bottles that <u>exploded</u> against the frozen pavement.

4. After two or three hours, I saw a man <u>working his way</u> toward me along the on-ramp from town.

5. He wore <u>filthy canvas</u> coveralls and carried a black lunch box, and as he got closer, I could see that his hair was <u>matted</u> in a way that occurs only after months <u>on the skids</u>.

6. In the <u>quickly gathering</u> dusk, I started walking back down the road looking for a place to spend the night.

E | **Critical Thinking: Applying.** Rewrite five of the sentences from your Free Writing using sensory details.

A | **Planning.** Follow the steps to make notes for your narrative.

Step 1 Look back at exercise **A** on page 204 and choose the story you want to tell.

Step 2 Write a thesis statement for your narrative in the space below. Answer the questions.

Step 3 Think about the beginning, the middle, and the end of your story. Use a time line like the one on page 202, if necessary. Then answer the questions to write a topic sentence for each of your body paragraphs.

Step 4 Note some ideas for an introduction. Include details that set the scene for your narrative, such as the time and place of your story.

Step 5 Think about ways to analyze and reflect on your life lesson for your conclusion. Restate your thesis and add some new information.

Introduction: Where/When did this happen? _____

Thesis statement: What did you learn? Why is this event important?

_____

1st body paragraph: What happened first?
Topic sentence: _____
Explanation and examples: _____
_____
_____

2nd body paragraph: Then what happened?
Topic sentence: _____
Explanation and examples: _____
_____
_____

3rd body paragraph: What happened after that?
Topic sentence: _____
Explanation and examples: _____
_____
_____

Optional additional body paragraphs: What happened after that?
Topic sentence: _____
Explanation and examples: _____
_____
_____

Conclusion: How/Why are these events important to you?
_____

B | **Draft 1.** Use your outline to write a first draft of your narrative.

When I was a child, my father had a saying: "All work is noble." What he meant was that it didn't matter what your job was—the important thing was to do your best at whatever you did. My parents weren't wealthy. They worked hard all their lives at honest, necessary jobs that I thought were dull. They provided a good life for me. Thanks to their efforts, I was able to go to college. But I wanted to do something different with my life, something glamorous—I was too special to take just any sort of job! But my attempts to get my dream job helped me to understand my father's words: "It doesn't matter what you do, just do the best you can."

It was January, in the middle of one of the coldest winters the East Coast had experienced in years. I had set out for New York to get a job as a graphic designer. I had studied design in college, and I had a great portfolio filled with samples of my work. I had a little money that I received as a graduation present. It was enough to get me there and to support myself for about a month. I was sure it would be enough—I would be offered a fantastic job immediately, or so I thought.

After a few weeks, though, I found myself wandering around the streets, down to my last few dollars. I had been to countless design offices, only to be turned away by one patronizing office flunky after another. I didn't get one interview. No one saw my work samples. I only had enough money for a couple more nights at the hostel where I was staying. I hadn't eaten since the previous day. I had no prospects and all the wrong clothes. How had I gotten to this point, I wondered as I shivered in my thin California jacket. But this was typical for me at the time. When I was in my early 20s, I thought I knew everything. It never occurred to me that I should have contacted design companies in advance, let alone checked the weather!

When I was just about to give up, I called my parents. I hadn't called them the entire time I was there—I was waiting until I had some good news. I felt that I should be supporting myself at this point in my life and not relying on other people—especially my parents—in any way. When I reached them, they suggested that I get a job working in a restaurant just until I could get something else. At first, I balked. I didn't come to New York to be a waiter. I could do that anywhere! I felt angry. I was disappointed in myself. But I was hungry, and I refused to go home feeling ashamed and defeated.

I decided that I wasn't going to give up. After that call, I gave some serious thought to what my parents had said. Earlier, I had noticed a posh-looking café near one of the design offices, and I headed over there. When I entered, I could see it was a popular place. There was a massive lunch crowd. A few harried waiters were dashing around carrying orders. I asked a woman at the front desk if they were hiring. She turned out to be the owner. She said they were shorthanded, and she offered me a job on the spot. To my surprise, I found that I was very good at being a waiter. I was completely amazed that I enjoyed serving people. I started making big tips right away and soon found a place to live. The main thing was that I felt good about myself—I was able to survive in a big city, and I didn't have to depend on my parents. Later, the owner learned that I had a design background. She paid me extra to design menus for the café. That work led to a part-time job at an advertising company.

A few weeks before, I never would have considered taking a job as a waiter, but there I was. I eventually got the design job of my dreams, but that winter I learned not to make assumptions about work. As my dad said, "All work is noble."

Step 1 What information does the introduction include to set up the story?

Step 2 Underline the thesis statement. Does it explain the lesson that the writer learned?

Step 3 Underline the time words and expressions that the writer used in the body paragraphs. Is the order of the events clear?

Step 4 Circle any sensory details in the narrative. Do they give you a clear picture of what the writer experienced?

Step 5 Does the writer analyze or reflect on the lesson in the conclusion?

D | **Revising.** Follow steps 1–5 in exercise **C** to analyze your own narrative.

E | **Peer Evaluation.** Exchange your first draft with a partner and follow these steps.

Step 1 Read your partner's narrative and tell him or her one thing that you liked about it.

Step 2 Complete the outline showing the information and events that your partner's narrative describes.

Introduction: Where/When did this happen? _____

Thesis statement: What did you learn? Why is this event important?

_____

1st body paragraph: What happened first?

Topic sentence: _____

Explanation and examples: _____

_____

_____

2nd body paragraph: Then what happened?

Topic sentence: _____

Explanation and examples: _____

_____

_____

3rd body paragraph: What happened after that?

Topic sentence: _____

Explanation and examples: _____

_____

_____

Optional additional body paragraphs: What happened after that?

Topic sentence: _____

Explanation and examples: _____

_____

_____

Conclusion: How/Why are these events important to you?

_____

Step 3 Compare this outline with the one that your partner created in exercise **A** on page 207.

Step 4 The two outlines should be similar. If they aren't, discuss how they differ.

F | Draft 2. Write a second draft of your narrative. Use what you learned from the peer evaluation activity and your answers to exercise **D**. Make any other necessary changes.

G | Editing Practice. Read the information in the box. Then find and correct one mistake in each sentence (1–4).

> When you use past forms, remember to use:
> - the past continuous for progressive actions in the past and the simple past for events that were completed: *I was walking along the trail when I met another hiker.*
> - the correct past participles in sentences with the past perfect. Memorize irregular past participles such as *buy* → *bought*. See page 250 for a list of past forms.

1. As soon as I arrived in Mexico City, I realized I had forgot all the Spanish I had ever learned.

2. I waited at the bus stop when a friendly-looking older man stopped and asked me if I wanted a ride.

3. I learned that I had not apply for a passport early enough to go on my trip at the end of the month.

4. I was looking for the exit when suddenly all the lights were going out.

H | Editing Checklist. Use the checklist to find errors in your second draft.

Editing Checklist	Yes	No
1. Are all the words spelled correctly?		
2. Does every sentence have correct punctuation?		
3. Do your subjects and verbs agree?		
4. Have you used past forms correctly?		

I | Final Draft. Now use your Editing Checklist to write a third draft of your narrative. Make any other necessary changes.

Imagining the Future

ACADEMIC PATHWAYS

Lesson A: Reading literature critically
Identifying literary elements

Lesson B: Writing critically about literature
Writing an analysis of fiction excerpts

UNIT

10

Think and Discuss

1. Do you think humans will ever live on another planet? Why, or why not?

2. Why do you think some people are fascinated with the idea of visiting other planets?

▲ An early science-fiction illustration by artist and explorer Anthony Fiala (1869–1950) depicts an imaginary trip to Mars.

Exploring the Theme

Read the information below and discuss the questions.

1. Why were a lot of science-fiction stories written in the 17th and 18th centuries?
2. Which of the books, television shows, and movies mentioned below have you read or seen? What others do you know about?
3. In what ways is modern science fiction different from that of previous centuries? How do you think science fiction will evolve in the future?

The origins of today's science-fiction tales can be traced back at least 2,000 years. The ancient Hindu epic *Ramayana* describes machines that can fly into space. The Greek playwright Aristophanes, who was alive at around the same time, also wrote about traveling through the air to other worlds—a dream that continues to inspire writers and filmmakers today.

8th–10th Centuries

In *One Thousand and One Nights*, also known as *The Arabian Nights*, the character Bulukiya travels through space to strange worlds in search of the herb of immortality.

17th and 18th Centuries

The period in Europe known as "The Age of Reason" was a time of great scientific discovery. Two notable stories of the period are English author Francis Godwin's *The Man in the Moone* (1638) and French writer Voltaire's *Micromégas* (1752), which suggested that people from other planets might be more advanced than people on Earth.

19th Century

Further scientific discoveries inspired stories of exploration under the sea, inside the earth, through time, and in outer space. Some of the most popular were Jules Verne's *From the Earth to the Moon* (1865) and H. G. Wells's *The War of the Worlds* (1898).

Early 20th Century

The creation of magazines devoted to science-fiction stories and the development of film technology led to a boom in science-fiction stories, ranging from Buck Rogers to Fritz Lang's 1927 movie *Metropolis*.

1940s to Today

Some of the best-known sci-fi stories—including Ray Bradbury's *The Martian Chronicles* (1950)— were written during the "Golden Age of Science Fiction" in the 1940s and 50s. Since then, the genre has evolved with TV shows, such as *Star Trek* and *The X-Files*, and movies about space exploration and invasion, such as *District 9* and *Avatar*.

▲ Michael Whelan's artwork for
The Martian Chronicles portrays
an imaginary alien landscape.

A | Building Vocabulary. Read the following paragraphs about science fiction. Use the context to guess the meanings of the words and phrase in **blue**. Then write the correct word or phrase to complete each sentence (1–6).

THE POWER OF SCIENCE FICTION

Ever since people first gazed up at the **flickering** stars, we have wondered what might be "out there." This fascination with distant worlds is still with us today. When we watch movies such as *Star Trek* or *Star Wars* and their many **sequels**, we can visit worlds that **look familiar** and strange at the same time. The alien **invasion** movie *Independence Day* speculated on our first encounters with intelligent—but unfriendly—beings. Science fiction also allows us to imagine the eventual **destiny** of our own planet: In the movie *Wall-E*, for example, a robot continues to clean up the Earth's trash, centuries after the last traces of humanity have **vanished** from our world.

James Cameron's *Avatar* ▶
envisaged a human-alien
clash of civilizations on a
distant planet.

1. If people or things _____ to you, they appear to be similar to someone or something that you know.

2. If people or things have _____, they have disappeared suddenly or in a way that cannot be explained.

3. A(n) _____ occurs when a foreign enemy enters a place, such as a country, by force.

4. _____ to a book or movie continue its story.

5. _____ refers to whatever will happen in the future, especially when it is considered to be controlled by someone or something else.

6. If a light or flame is _____, it is shining unsteadily.

B | Building Vocabulary. Complete the definitions (1–6) with the words or phrase from the box. Use a dictionary to help you.

dwindle	flee	in proportion	literally	resembles	stunned

1. If one thing or person _____ another, the two things or people are very similar to each other.

2. If you _____ a person or thing, you escape from that person or thing.

3. If you are _____ by something, you are extremely shocked or surprised by it.

4. If one thing increases or decreases _____ to another thing, it changes to the same degree as the second item.

5. You use "_____" to emphasize that what you are saying is true, even though it seems exaggerated or surprising.

6. If things _____, they become smaller, weaker, or fewer in number.

Word Link

liter = letter: alliteration, illiterate, literal, literally

Word Partners

Use **flee/fled** with nouns: (*n.*) fled **the scene**; (*from + n.*) fled **from the situation**, (*to + n.*) fled **to safety**

C | Using Vocabulary. Answer the questions. Share your ideas with a partner.

1. Think of a movie or television show that portrays life on a distant planet. In what ways does the world **resemble** our own world? How is it different?

2. What technology that we use today do you think will **vanish** in 10, 20, or 50 years? What kinds of technology do you think we will have instead?

3. What do you think is the **destiny** of our own planet? What will it be like 1,000 years from now?

D | Brainstorming. Discuss these questions in a small group.

1. What are some reasons that someone might want to write stories about space exploration?

2. What are some reasons that humans might want to live on another planet?

E | Predicting. Skim the reading passages on pages 216–222 and answer the questions. As you read, check your predictions.

1. What kind of reading is the first passage (pages 216–218)?

   a. a fictional story
   b. an autobigraphical essay
   c. an explanatory article

2. What kind of reading is the second passage (pages 219–222)?

   a. a set of fictional stories
   b. extracts from an autobiography
   c. explanatory articles

MY MARS

by Ray Bradbury

"That was the day Mars took me home— and I never really came back. "

track 2-05

A WHEN I WAS SIX YEARS OLD, I moved to Tucson, Arizona, and lived on Lowell Avenue, little realizing I was on an avenue that led to Mars. It was named for the great astronomer Percival Lowell, who took fantastic photographs of the planet that promised a spacefaring future to children like myself.

B Along the way to growing up, I read Edgar Rice Burroughs and loved his Martian books, and followed the instructions of his Mars pioneer John Carter, who told me, when I was 12, that it was simple: If I wanted to follow the avenue of Lowell and go to the stars, I needed to go out on the summer night lawn, lift my arms, stare at the planet Mars, and say, "Take me home."

C That was the day that Mars took me home—and I never really came back. I began writing on a toy typewriter. I couldn't afford to buy all the Martian books I wanted, so I wrote the **sequels** myself.

D When I was 15, a Martian disguised as an American boy went to see the film *Things to Come*, by H. G. Wells, about a dark, war-torn future Earth. In the final scene the protagonist,[1] Cabal, and his friend Passworthy watch the first moon rocket disappear into the heavens carrying their two grown children toward a brighter **destiny**. Cabal looks toward the dust at his feet then up at the stars, saying to Passworthy and to the audience, "Is it this or that? All the universe or nothing? Which shall it be? Which shall it be?"

E This Martian staggered out of the theater inspired to write more stories because I knew we were going to the stars.

F Some years later, I made my way to New York City on a Greyhound bus, hoping to find a publisher. I carried a bundle of manuscripts with me, and people would ask, "Is that a novel?" To which I replied, "No, I write short stories." On my last night in New York, I got a break. I had dinner with an editor from Doubleday who said to me, "I think that without realizing it, you have, in fact, written a novel."

G I asked him what he meant.

H He replied, "If you tied all your Martian landscapes together and made a tapestry of them, wouldn't they make a book that you could call *The Martian Chronicles*?"

I I was **stunned.** The small Martian in me hadn't realized that he'd been putting his hands inside my hands and moving the typewriter keys to write a book. I finished it over the next six months. I was 29—and well on my way to the stars.

[1] The **protagonist** of a story is the main character.

▲ A view from one of the *Viking* landers, which touched down on Mars in 1976

J In 1976 I was invited to stay overnight at the Jet Propulsion Laboratory in Pasadena, waiting for news to come back from the *Viking 1* lander, which was going to touch down on Mars and take photographs.

K It was incredibly exciting to be there, surrounded by engineers, waiting for the first pictures. There was a tall gentleman standing next to me, who I thought **looked familiar**. At last, I realized it was none other than Wernher von Braun, the man who had **fled** Germany for America to become the co-inventor of the rocket that took us to the moon and that was now taking us to the planets.

L Early in the morning, the photographs began to arrive. I could hardly believe I was seeing the surface of Mars! At 9:00 A.M., ABC television put me on the air to get my reaction.

M The interviewer said, "Mr. Bradbury, how do you feel about this landing? Where are the Martian cities and where are all the living beings?"

N "Don't be a fool," I said. "WE are the Martians! We're going to be here for the next million years. At long last, WE ARE MARTIANS!"

O That was the end of the interview.

P **I LIKE TO THINK** of the cosmos[2] as a theater, yet a theater cannot exist without an audience, to witness and to celebrate. Robot craft and mighty telescopes will continue to show us unimaginable wonders. But when humans return to the moon and put a base there and prepare to go to Mars and become true Martians, we—the audience—**literally** enter the cosmic theater. Will we finally reach the stars?

Q A few years ago, I traveled back to my boyhood home in Tucson. I stood out on the lawn and looked up at the night sky—and realized the stars had never looked closer than right there on Lowell Avenue.

[2] The **cosmos** is the universe.

AUGUST 2001 THE SETTLERS

The men of Earth came to Mars

They came because they were afraid or unafraid, because they were happy or unhappy, because they felt like Pilgrims or did not feel like Pilgrims. There was a reason for each man. They were leaving bad wives or bad jobs or bad towns; they were coming to find something or leave something or get something, to dig up something or bury something or leave something alone. They were coming with small dreams or large dreams or none at all. But a government finger pointed from four-color posters in many towns: THERE'S WORK FOR YOU IN THE SKY: SEE MARS! and the men shuffled forward, only a few at first, a doublescore,[3] for most men felt the great illness in them even before the rocket fired into space. And this disease was called The Loneliness, because when you saw your home town **dwindle** to the size of your fist and then lemon-size and then pin-size and **vanish** in the fire-wake, you felt you had never been born, there was no town, you were nowhere, with space all around, nothing familiar, only other strange men. And when the state of Illinois, Iowa, Missouri, or Montana vanished into cloud seas, and, doubly, when the United States shrank to a misted island and the entire planet Earth became a muddy baseball tossed away, then you were alone, wandering in the meadows of space, on your way to a place you couldn't imagine.

So it was not unusual that the first men were few. The number grew steadily **in proportion** to the census of Earth Men already on Mars. There was comfort in numbers. But the first Lonely Ones had to stand by themselves.

[3] A score is 20 or about 20, so a **doublescore** is about 40.

FEBRUARY 2002 THE LOCUSTS

The rockets set the bony meadows afire, turned rock to lava, turned wood to charcoal, transmitted water to steam, made sand and silica into green glass which lay like shattered mirrors reflecting the **invasion**, all about. The rockets came like drums, beating in the night. The rockets came like locusts,[4] swarming and settling in blooms of rosy smoke. And from the rockets ran men with hammers in their hands to beat the strange world into a shape that was familiar to the eye, to bludgeon away all the strangeness, their mouths fringed with nails so they **resembled** steel-toothed carnivores, spitting them into their swift hands as they hammered up frame cottages and scuttled over roofs with shingles to blot out the eerie stars, and fit green shades to pull against the night. And when the carpenters had hurried on, the women came in with flowerpots and chintz[5] and pans and set up a kitchen clamor to cover the silence that Mars made waiting outside the door and the shaded window.

In six months a dozen small towns had been laid down upon the naked planet, filled with sizzling neon tubes and yellow electric bulbs. In all, some ninety thousand people came to Mars, and more, on Earth, were packing their grips. . . . [6]

[4] **Locusts** are large insects, similar to grasshoppers, that live mainly in hot areas and often cause serious damage to crops.
[5] **Chintz** is a cotton fabric decorated with flowery patterns.
[6] **Grips** are small suitcases.

NOVEMBER 2005 THE WATCHERS

They all came out and looked at the sky that night. They left their suppers or their washing up or their dressing for the show and they came out upon their now-not-quite-as-new porches and watched the green star of Earth there. It was a move without conscious effort; they all did it, to help them understand the news they had heard on the radio a moment before. There was Earth and there the coming war, and there hundreds of thousands of mothers or grandmothers or fathers or brothers or aunts or uncles or cousins. They stood on the porches and tried to believe in the existence of Earth, much as they had once tried to believe in the existence of Mars; it was a problem reversed. To all intents and purposes, Earth now was dead; they had been away from it for three or four years. Space was an anesthetic; seventy million miles of space numbed you, put memory to sleep, depopulated Earth, erased the past, and allowed these people here to go on with their work. But now, tonight, the dead were risen, Earth was reinhabited, memory awoke, a million names were spoken: What was so-and-so doing tonight on Earth? What about this one and that one? The people on the porches glanced sidewise at each other's faces.

At nine o'clock Earth seemed to explode, catch fire, and burn.

The people on the porches put up their hands as if to beat the fire out.

They waited.

By midnight the fire was extinguished. Earth was still there.
There was a sigh, like an autumn wind, from the porches.

"We haven't heard from Harry for a long time."

"He's all right."

"We should send a message to Mother."

"She's all right."

"Is she?"

"Now, don't worry."

"Will she be all right, do you think?"

"Of course, of course; now come to bed."

But nobody moved. Late dinners were carried out onto the night lawns and set upon collapsible tables, and they picked at these slowly until two o'clock and the light-radio message flashed from Earth. They could read the great Morse-code flashes which **flickered** like a distant firefly:

AUSTRALIAN CONTINENT ATOMIZED IN PREMATURE EXPLOSION OF ATOMIC STOCKPILE. LOS ANGELES, LONDON BOMBED. WAR. COME HOME. COME HOME. COME HOME.

Continued on page 222

They stood up from their tables.

COME HOME. COME HOME. COME HOME.

"Have you heard from your brother Ted this year?"

"You know. With mail rates five bucks a letter to Earth, I don't write much."

COME HOME.

Z "I've been wondering about Jane; you remember Jane, my kid sister?"

COME HOME.

At three in the chilly morning, the luggage-store proprietor glanced up.
A lot of people were coming down the street.

"Stayed open late on purpose. What'll it be, mister?"

By dawn the luggage was gone from his shelves.

Reading Skill: Identifying Literary Elements

Literary fiction consists of several elements. These are similar to the elements of a personal narrative (see page 202).

Plot: the action of the story—what the characters do, say, and think. Plot has a beginning, a middle, and an end. Between the beginning and the middle, action rises toward the story's climax, or most intense point. After that, the action falls toward the conclusion, or resolution, of the story.

Characters: all of the individuals in the story. These can include people, animals, or any other things that perform action or express thoughts in the story. The main character of a story is called the protagonist.

Setting: the time and place (when and where) the story takes place. However, the setting is more than just a time and location; it can also set the mood for a story.

Point of view: the perspective from which the story is told. Is the story told by a narrator outside of the story? Is it told by a character?

Theme: the story's main idea or central message. A story can have more than one theme. Sometimes the theme is stated directly, and other times it is implied.

A | Analyzing. Match each element below with an example from *The Martian Chronicles*.

Element

1. _____ plot
2. _____ characters
3. _____ setting
4. _____ point of view
5. _____ theme

Example

a. narrator (the writer of the story)
b. human colonists
c. the effects of colonization
d. People who have moved from Earth to Mars watch the Earth, anticipating a war. Eventually, they see parts of the Earth blow up. They decide to go back to Earth.
e. small towns set up on the surface of Mars

B | Applying. Complete the chart with information about a story you have read or a movie you have seen. Then describe the story to a partner.

Title	
Main Character (Protagonist)	
Setting	
Point of View	
Theme(s)	
Plot	

A | Understanding Main Ideas. Write answers to the questions about "My Mars" on pages 216–218. Share your ideas with a partner.

1. What events or experiences in Ray Bradbury's childhood led to his writing *The Martian Chronicles*?

_____

_____

_____

2. Bradbury writes that "WE are the Martians!" (paragraph N). What does he mean?

_____

_____

_____

B | Identifying Key Details. Write answers to the questions about "My Mars."

1. Who is John Carter? What influence did he have on Bradbury?

_____

_____

2. Why did Bradbury write sequels to the books that he read?

_____

_____

3. Why was Bradbury's visit to Pasadena in 1976 significant?

_____

_____

C | Identifying Meaning from Context. Find and underline the following words and phrases in the reading. Use context to match each word or phrase with its meaning.

1. _____ Paragraph B: **along the way**   a. walked very unsteadily

2. _____ Paragraph E: **staggered**   b. was lucky after a period of effort

3. _____ Paragraph F: **got a break**   c. after you have been hoping for it for a long time

4. _____ Paragraph J: **touch down**   d. during the course of a particular event or process

5. _____ Paragraph K: **none other than**   e. in fact; surprisingly

6. _____ Paragraph N: **at long last**   f. land (an aircraft or a spacecraft) on the ground

The first time you read a short story or novel, you can simply enjoy it and pay attention to the events in the story. When you read it again, you can focus more on the characters, plot, theme, and language. As you read, ask yourself questions: *Why do the characters do the things they do? How can I compare the elements in the story to elements in real life? What do people and things in the story symbolize? What is the author's message?*

D | **Critical Thinking: Reading Literature Critically.** Write notes to answer the questions about the excerpts on pages 219–222. Then discuss your answers in a small group.

THE SETTLERS

1. What event causes "The Loneliness"? What real-life event can you compare with The Loneliness?

   _____

   _____

2. The narrator explains that people came to Mars "because they were afraid or unafraid, because they were happy or unhappy, . . . " How might two people with opposite reasons for leaving Earth make the same decision—to go to Mars?

   _____

   _____

   _____

THE LOCUSTS

3. Why do you think the first excerpt is titled "THE LOCUSTS"? Who or what are the locusts in the story?

   _____

   _____

4. The men from the rockets ran "with hammers in their hands to beat the strange world into a shape that was familiar to the eye." Why did they do this? In what ways do people do this in the real world?

   _____

   _____

THE WATCHERS

5. What emotions are the colonists experiencing? What do they decide to do? How do we know this?

   _____

   _____

E | **Critical Thinking: Interpreting Figurative Language.** Read each sentence or phrase (1–7) from the reading. What is Bradbury saying in each case? Why does he use figurative language rather than literal language? Discuss your ideas with a partner.

MY MARS

1. That was the day that Mars took me home—and I never really came back.

2. The small Martian in me hadn't realized that he'd been putting his hands inside my hands and moving the typewriter keys to write a book.

THE SETTLERS

3. And this disease was called The Loneliness, because when you saw your home town dwindle . . . you felt you had never been born, there was no town, you were nowhere, with space all around, nothing familiar, only other strange men.

THE LOCUSTS

4. The rockets came like drums, beating in the night.

5. . . . their mouths fringed with nails so they resembled steel-toothed carnivores . . .

THE WATCHERS

6. They could read the great Morse-code flashes which flickered like a distant firefly.

7. Space was an anesthetic.

F | **Critical Thinking: Making Inferences.** Write answers to the questions.

1. Based on what Bradbury writes in "My Mars," why do you think he told the kinds of stories that he told?

_____

_____

_____

_____

2. What is one message or warning that you think Bradbury was trying to communicate with his stories?

_____

_____

_____

_____

MISSION: MARS

Before Viewing

A | Using a Dictionary. Here are some words you will hear in the video. Match each word with the correct definition. Use your dictionary to help you.

1. _____: a deep crack in something, especially in rock or in the ground

2. _____: very large

3. _____: the land, water, or plants that you can see around you

4. _____: the force that causes things to fall toward a large object, such as a planet

> colossal
> fissure
> gravity
> scenery

B | Thinking Ahead. If you could visit Mars, what do you think you would see? Make a list with a partner.

_____

_____

While Viewing

A | Watch the video about Mars. As you watch, check your answer to exercise **B** above. Circle the things that are mentioned.

B | Read questions 1–4. Think about the answers as you view the video.

1. What is the Valles Marineris?
2. What is significant about the fissure at the bottom of the Valles Marineris?
3. How much higher is the Mons Olympus than Mount Everest?
4. How might the gravity on Mars affect the height of the Mons Olympus?

After Viewing

A | Discuss your answers to questions 1–4 above with a partner.

B | Critical Thinking: Synthesizing. Imagine that Ray Bradbury had today's current knowledge of Mars when he wrote *The Martian Chronicles*. How do you think the knowledge might have affected his stories?

▼ Victoria Crater, Mars

GOAL: Writing an Analysis of Literature

In this lesson, you are going to plan, write, revise, and edit a paper on the following topic:
Write an analysis of the three excerpts from The Martian Chronicles.

Writing Skill: Writing Critically about Literature

When you write an analysis of a story or novel, you choose one aspect of the story or novel to focus on. Then you state an argument about that aspect, and you use quotes and paraphrases from the story as evidence to support your argument. The argument should be broad enough that you can write several paragraphs about it.

Good argument/question: In *The Martian Chronicles*, Ray Bradbury shows us that when we try to escape from our problems, we do not suddenly have perfect and happy lives.

Weak argument/question: In *The Martian Chronicles*, people decide to go to Mars to escape their problems.

In each paragraph of your analysis, you can include one or more quotes or paraphrases from the story as your evidence. Then show how each of the quotes or paraphrases is significant. In other words, show how it supports your argument or answer.

A | Critical Thinking: Evaluating. Check (✓) the statements that are possible topics for analysis of *The Martian Chronicles*.

☐ 1. The actions and feelings of the people in *The Martian Chronicles* are similar to the actions and experiences of people in real life in several ways.

☐ 2. In "November 2005: THE WATCHERS," the people are watching a war on Earth.

☐ 3. Many events in *The Martian Chronicles* are similar to events that occur in real life.

☐ 4. In many ways, *The Martian Chronicles* is a cautionary tale for readers.

☐ 5. *The Martian Chronicles* is a famous story about space exploration.

B | Critical Thinking: Evaluating. Check (✓) four pieces of evidence that best support the following argument: *In* The Martian Chronicles, *Ray Bradbury shows us that when we try to escape from our problems, we do not suddenly have perfect and happy lives.*

☐ 1. The government wanted workers to move to Mars.

☐ 2. "And this disease was called The Loneliness, because when you saw your home town dwindle, you were nowhere, with space all around, nothing familiar, only other strange men."

3. ☐ "The number grew steadily in proportion to the census of Earth Men already on Mars."

4. ☐ The rockets burned up and destroyed the land as they invaded Mars.

5. ☐ "the women . . . set up a kitchen clamor to cover the silence that Mars made waiting outside the door and shaded window."

6. ☐ "AUSTRALIAN CONTINENT ATOMIZED IN PREMATURE EXPLOSION OF ATOMIC STOCKPILE. LOS ANGELES, LONDON BOMBED. WAR. COME HOME. COME HOME. COME HOME."

7. ☐ "They stood up from their tables."

Language for Writing: Using a Variety of Sentence Types

One way to add interest to your writing is to include a variety of sentence types: simple, compound, and complex.

A simple sentence consists of one independent clause (one subject and verb).

The men went to Mars.

A compound sentence consists of two independent clauses joined by a coordinating conjunction (*for, and, or, but, so, nor, yet*).

People wanted to escape their problems, so they went to Mars.

A complex sentence consists of at least one independent clause and one or more dependent clauses. Dependent clauses begin with relative pronouns such as *that*, *who*, or *which*, or with subordinating conjunctions such as *because*, *although*, *before*, *after*, or *when*.

Using only simple sentences can make your writing sound abrupt or choppy. However, if you combine those sentences, your writing will sound smoother.

The men landed on Mars. They changed the landscape. They wanted it to look like Earth.

↓

After they landed on Mars, the men changed the landscape so that it looked like Earth.

C | Analyzing. What kind of sentence is each of the following? Write **S** for simple, **CD** for compound, or **CX** for complex.

1. _____ The individuals from Earth go to Mars for various reasons, but many go to leave problems behind such as "bad wives or bad jobs or bad towns."

2. _____ However, some of them eventually find that they're leaving one set of problems for another.

3. _____ In "February 2002: THE LOCUSTS," as more and more rockets land on their new home planet, they burn the planet's trees and meadows and melt the rock and sand.

4. _____ They turn Mars into a second Earth "filled with sizzling neon tubes and yellow electric bulbs."

5. _____ In a sense, they bring their problems with them because they need to be surrounded by familiar things such as "flowerpots and chintz" on this strange new planet.

D | **Brainstorming.** Brainstorm ideas from the three excerpts from *The Martian Chronicles* on pages 219–222 that support each of the arguments below.

1. The actions and feelings of the people in *The Martian Chronicles* are similar to the actions and experiences of people in real life in several ways. (Consider the following: the reasons for going to Mars, the colonization of Mars, the war, the desire to return to Earth.)

_____

_____

_____

_____

_____

2. In many ways, *The Martian Chronicles* is a cautionary tale for readers. (Consider the following: people who want to escape their problems, wars, and governments that want to colonize other countries.)

_____

_____

_____

_____

_____

Free Writing. Write for five minutes. Choose one of the arguments from exercise **A**. Write down any details and ideas that might help you support the argument.

A | **Planning.** Follow the steps to make notes for your paper.

Step 1   Decide the argument from exercise **A** (page 228) you will write about. Write your thesis statement in the outline below.

Step 2   Reread the three excerpts from *The Martian Chronicles* on pages 219–222. Underline any parts of the story that might support your thesis.

Step 3   Write the topic sentences for your three body paragraphs.

Step 4   Write notes about evidence from the excerpts that support each topic sentence. For each piece of evidence, write notes about why the evidence is significant.

Introductory paragraph: What is your argument?

_____

_____

1st body paragraph: What is one piece of evidence that supports your thesis?

Topic sentence: _____

_____

Evidence and significance of evidence: _____

_____

2nd body paragraph: What is a second piece of evidence that supports your thesis?

Topic sentence: _____

_____

Evidence and significance of evidence: _____

_____

3rd body paragraph: What is a third piece of evidence that supports your thesis?

Topic sentence: _____

_____

Evidence and significance of evidence: _____

_____

Concluding paragraph: Review your main points and your thesis statement.

_____

_____

B | **Draft 1.** Use your outline to write a first draft of your analytical paper.

Use italics for the titles of books and movies.

The Martian Chronicles is a novel about a time when humans on Earth start moving to and colonizing the planet Mars. The individuals from Earth go to Mars for various reasons, but many go to leave problems behind such as "bad wives or bad jobs or bad towns." However, some of them eventually find that they're leaving one set of problems for another. In *The Martian Chronicles*, Ray Bradbury shows us that when we try to escape from our problems, we don't suddenly have perfect and happy lives.

When you write about literature, use the present tense.

The first problem that moving to Mars causes for the migrants is a disease called "The Loneliness." As the narrator explains in "August 2001: THE SETTLERS," "this disease was called The Loneliness, because when you saw your home town dwindle to the size of your fist . . . you felt you had never been born, there was no town, you were nowhere, with space all around, nothing familiar, only other strange men." This shows that the migrants are creating new problems for themselves as they try to escape their old problems. At least on Earth, people were surrounded by familiarity—a town they knew, people they knew, and people who knew them. On their way to Mars, the "Lonely Ones" become nothing and are surrounded by nothing.

You can weave quotes from the story into your own sentences.

Another problem that the migrants experience is the ugliness of their own invasion of Mars. In "February 2002: THE LOCUSTS," as more and more rockets land on their new home planet, they burn the planet's trees and meadows and melt the rock and sand. And even though many of the migrants come to Mars to escape their lives on Earth, they recreate some of the less appealing things on Earth. They turn Mars into a second Earth "filled with sizzling neon tubes and yellow electric bulbs." This demonstrates that in a sense, they bring their problems with them because they need to be surrounded by familiar things such as "flowerpots and chintz" on this strange new planet.

Use quotation marks around chapter titles and poem titles.

In "November 2005: THE WATCHERS," the migrants learn that they really can't escape their own problems or their own lives. For a while, they are able to forget about Earth. After being on Mars for three or four years, "Earth now was dead" to them. However, as they watch Earth seem to "explode, catch fire, and burn" at the start of a war, they are reminded of the people and the lives they left behind. They start to wonder and worry about them. When they receive a message telling them to "COME HOME. COME HOME. COME HOME," they feel that they have to. This supports the idea that their problems haven't disappeared. They need to go back to Earth and reclaim the lives that they abandoned.

Through the actions and words of the characters in the story, Ray Bradbury's *The Martian Chronicles* shows the reader that even if you go to another planet, you can't forget about who you are or live a problem-free life. No matter where you go, you bring your problems with you, or you create new ones.

Step 1 Underline the thesis statement.

Step 2 Underline the topic sentences of the body paragraphs.

Step 3 Circle each piece of evidence in the body paragraphs.

Step 4 Underline the main points that are reviewed in the conclusion.

D | **Revising.** Follow the steps in exercise **C** to analyze your own analytical paper.

E | **Peer Evaluation.** Exchange your first draft with a partner and follow these steps.

Step 1 Read your partner's analytical paper and tell him or her one thing that you liked about it.

Step 2 Complete the outline showing the ideas that your partner's paper describes.

Introductory paragraph: What is your partner's argument?

_____

_____

1st body paragraph: What is one piece of evidence that supports the thesis?

Topic sentence: _____

_____

Evidence and significance of evidence: _____

_____

2nd body paragraph: What is a second piece of evidence that supports the thesis?

Topic sentence: _____

_____

Evidence and significance of evidence: _____

_____

3rd body paragraph: What is a third piece of evidence that supports the thesis?

Topic sentence: _____

_____

Evidence and significance of evidence: _____

_____

Concluding paragraph: Review the main points and thesis statement.

_____

_____

Step 3 Compare this outline with the one that your partner created in exercise **A** on page 231.

Step 4 The two outlines should be similar. If they aren't, discuss how they differ.

F | Draft 2. Write a second draft of your analytical paper. Use what you learned from the peer evaluation activity and your answers to exercise **D**. Make any other necessary changes.

G | Editing Practice. Use the checklist to find errors in your second draft.

Editing Checklist	Yes	No
1. Are all the words spelled correctly?		
2. Does every sentence have correct punctuation?		
3. Do your subjects and verbs agree?		
4. Have you used a variety of sentence types?		
5. Are your verb tenses correct?		

H | Final Draft. Now use your Editing Checklist to write a third draft of your paper. Make any other necessary changes.

◄ A Martian greets a human visitor in a scene from the TV adaptation of *The Martian Chronicles*.

Kenyans in New York

Boniface Kandari Parsulan: After long flight from Africa, we wanted to get out and stretch our legs, and then he said, "Come on, I'll show you around my village."

Rene Lopez: Follow my lead, follow my lead.

Loyapan Lemarti: Yes, boss.

Boni: Village? This not what I call a village!

Rene: Check it out.

Boni: Some people are living on top of that?

Rene: Yeah. An apartment—there on top, that's the second floor, third floor, fourth floor. So, we live on top of each other.

Boni: Because there's no place to live or what? Why do people go up there?

Rene: There's no land, so you have to live on top of each other. So? So you keep building and building and building, up, up, up, up.

Loyapan: One very important thing we need to do first. If you going to walk on the street, you must have dollar.

Rene: All right, here we go, guys. ATM. This is where I get my money.

Loyapan: Hoooo!!

Rene: Voila!

Loyapan: What's *voila*?

Rene: Well, . . .

Boni: You take someone else money?

Rene: There you go. No, I'm not takin—this is my money.

Boni: So, you always put your money here?

Rene: It's from my bank account.

Boni: So, people can break it here easily and get your money here, here?

Rene: Yes.

Boni: Why do you put your money here?

Loyapan: Where Boni and I come from, we trade things to get money. Our ATM, it's a goat. We take a goat to the market, we sell it, we get money. No dollars coming from the wall. I think dollar talk in America very much, you know. You have no dollar, you have no voice (*tsk, tsk*).

Rene: Yeah, I wish I could fully explain it to you, but I can't.

Boni: Easy money, easy money, easy!

Loyapan: What this place, Randy?

Rene: This is Washington Square Park.

Loyapan: We're walking through the, through the park. It's a lot of people sitting around eating, drinking, chilling. You know, people eat a lot here, people graze like cows, man. You know? Nonstop. Every corner you go, you see somebody sitting down eating. Randy said, "Hey, let's grab something to eat, guys."

Rene: All right, so we're gonna order a hot dog.

Boni: What kind of a dogs (*stutters*) does they sell?

Rene: Hot dogs. Beef.

Boni: Beef? Yes. OK.

Rene: Can we have one hot dog, please? With mustard and ketchup on it.

Loyapan: You can't even tell if this is a meat or what.

Boni: Randy, what's inside this hot dog? What's that, inside the hot dog?

Rene: It's ah, a smooshed-up cow.

Loyapan: Boni just like (*action*) to the hot dog, and say "Oh yeah." I want take one home to show people that what Boni ate.

Boni: Are you sure, are you sure, Randy, this is a, a cow? Is that New York style?

Rene: That's New York style. Say again. Let's hear you. (*starts skatting*) hot dog! (*skatting "boom, bap"*) hot dog!

All together: *Boom, bap, hot dog!*

The Encroaching Desert

Narrator: It is hard to believe that 4,000 years ago the Sahara was a fertile region. Today, it's the largest desert in the world.

Desertification is destroying increasing amounts of farmland because of the combined actions of drought and human activity. The Sahel region of Africa, which extends from Senegal to the Sudan, is one of the regions most seriously affected by desertification.

Once, monsoon rains maintained wild vegetation that protected the ground from the sun and formed a barrier against drying winds. In the last half-century, however, previously nomadic peoples have built permanent towns and intensified their agricultural activities. The soil has been overused and become sterile. Desertification is a problem on every continent.

The Aral Sea, in Asia, has been drying up since 1954 because the rivers that once fed it have been diverted to irrigate cotton fields. In the space of 40 years, the Aral Sea lost sixty percent of its area; it is now reduced to two lakes.

On the planetary scale, it is estimated that 5 to 6 million hectares of farmland become desertified every year.

Secrets of a Long Life

Residents of Sardinia, Okinawa, and Loma Linda, California, live longer, healthier lives than just about anyone else on Earth. To understand the reasons behind this, David McLain travelled to these three different cultures of longevity. He spent time in each of these places and tried to learn about their cultures of longevity. He learned about what it is they are doing to live vital and healthy lives well into their hundreds.

The first longevity hotspot he traveled to was Sardinia, Italy. What is phenomenal about this region is that men are living just as long as women. Science isn't exactly quite sure why, but one theory is that it's because women are in charge of family finances and household management, as well as child rearing. So, men have less stress as a result. Also, the Sardinians have a fanatical zeal for the family. David witnessed one family of four generations coming together to share a giant meal, which they do every weekend. David reflected, "This is what being alive and having a family is all about." This social component of longevity is incredibly important.

However, the cultures of longevity in Sardinia are rapidly disappearing. Unfortunately, the Sardinians are moving away from traditional, natural food and are leading a sedentary lifestyle. He spent time with a woman who was almost a hundred, and her great-granddaughter. Later that day he saw that same great-granddaughter eating potato chips, and wondered, "Will the next generation live as long?"

Okinawa is an archipelago in the far south of Japan. It is home to the longest-lived people on Earth. There, David met numerous people who were into their hundreds, and they were leading active and very healthy lifestyles. The 90-year-olds were biking and fishing eight miles offshore using old diving techniques on the reef. He met an amazing woman who was over a hundred. She had been in a moai.

The rough translation of the word is a group of friends who go through life together and help each other. David believes the energy and vitality that they would get from that factored into the longevity equation. The Okinawans have a wonderful word called ikigai. It translates roughly into the reason for which you wake up in the morning. All of the centenarians had ikigai, yet another reason why so many Okinawans are living so long. One of the cornerstones of Okinawan longevity is caloric restriction. Yet, interestingly, they are eating a lot of food. The trick is that the foods that they are eating are all low in caloric density. The food included beautiful miso soups filled with carrots, seaweed, onions, and potatoes. Like the Sardinians, the Okinawans grew most of the food themselves; in their gardens . . . they go to the store for very little.

Still, Okinawa is losing its longevity edge. Okinawa has the highest rate of obesity in all of Japan. For David, this was quite shocking and somewhat disturbing to see this culture of longevity disappearing right before his eyes.

One of the most surprising facts that David discovered from his research is that a community of Seventh-day Adventists outlive their American counterparts by about 10 years. What are they doing? Quite simply, the Seventh-day Adventists, who largely populate Loma Linda, California, have a religion that reinforces positive, healthy behaviors. For example, if you are a devout Seventh-day Adventist, you are a vegetarian, nondrinker, nonsmoker, and take every Saturday off to do nothing but relax and unwind. He met several incredible people including a woman who had just turned a hundred and renewed her driver's license.

Before he could go with her for a cruise, she had to go through her morning routine, where she lifts weights and rides a stationary bike. Interestingly, the Seventh-day Adventists are the only culture of longevity that he visited who are not losing their longevity edge. While photographing a baptism at the church, David thought about how this was the perfect example of the way this culture is still growing while maintaining their traditions.

Frontline Diary

Narrator: Afghanistan, remote, majestic and shrouded in mystery.

Sebastian Junger: It's one of the most inaccessible places in the world.

Narrator: It's a land of deadly violence.

Reza Deghati: We have to go, they have seen us.

Sebastian: Hate this part.

Narrator: For two journalists, one a veteran photograph, the other a best-selling writer, the danger is part of the job. They can only tell this story by jumping in to the chaos and experiencing it all—from haunting tragedies, to the inspiring optimism of people who won't give up hope, because finding Afghanistan's soul is the only way to figure out its future.

Narrator: Reza and Sebastian meet for the first time at the Munich airport.

Sebastian: Reza, Hey.

Reza: Hi, Sebastian.

Sebastian: Good to meet you.

Reza: How are you? Good to meet you.

Narrator: Their final destination—Afghanistan, a place where the odds between surviving and dying are often even money.

Narrator: Massoud has offered to smuggle Sebastian and Reza into the country, but they have to go before the sun sets.

Sebastian: That can't be the helicopter.

Reza: This is it.

Sebastian: It looks like it's been rusting for years.

Reza: No, no, this is it, this is the helicopter.

Narrator: If everything goes right it would take but an hour to reach the warzone but a lot could go wrong. An aging helicopter will be flying over Taliban airspace and will be no match for enemy jets. With no radar, they have to clear the mountains while there is still light or they will be forced to turn back. As they begin their decent they are in total darkness. They finally land with only the help of car headlights.

Sebastian: It was like being in an old truck, except it flew.

Reza: I really feel very, very, good now being here.

Narrator: Day 1, Massoud's local headquarters, Reza begins his day, just like any other, with Tai Chi. But Sebastian isn't as lucky.

Reza: Have they bring in tea? How do you feel now?

Sebastian: I feel better. The aspirin's in. It's part of the job, practically. I don't think I've ever gone to a 3rd world and not getting sick.

Narrator: At breakfast Sebastian is already gathering details for his story. This sort of beautiful formality of eating breakfast in the morning. You don't eat it out of cereal bowl and watch TV. You know there is a ritual. By mid-morning Reza and Sebastian find their way to a make-shift refugee camp along the Kokcha River. What they are about to see, won't be forgotten. Roughly 750,000 people have been driven from homes in this country, making Afghanistan the center of the world's worst refugee crisis.

Sebastian: The thing that really makes an impression sometimes is this incredible generosity of these people. You meet Afghans and they welcome you into their home; they'll give you their last crust of bread. It's very, very, moving.

Mission: Mars

Dr. Steve Squyres: You know if you are going to Mars you'd want to go for the scenery, right? I mean you're not going for the culture; you're not going for the climate, so you definitely want to go for the scenery.

One thing that people forget is that when we've landed on Mars, we have to go to places that are safe, and safe equals pretty smooth and flat.

Narrator: Here's a bit of Mars that's anything but smooth and flat. The magnificent Valles Marineris. This titanic canyon system, over two and a half thousand miles long, and six miles deep, is probably the grandest geological feature in the solar system. It's clearly the red planet's must see destination.

Dr. David Southwood: As a human being, it's the sheer gigantism of Mars that is amazing. The Valles Marineris, is, beats the Grand Canyon, hollow, and if you've ever seen the Grand Canyon you will never forget it.

Narrator: It's so colossal; the Grand Canyon would be easily swallowed by one of the smaller side branches.

Scientist 1: We're talking about something here that's the width of the United States or of Australia crossed here.

Dr. Steve Squyres: See I think the Valles Marineris would, would be the space to go. I mean build a lodge right on the rim so you can look in.

Narrator: The attraction goes beyond sheer scenic splendor. Deeper than the canyon itself, is the mystery surrounding its formation. This giant fissure, once filled by mighty lakes, has been scoured by floods of biblical proportions.

Scientist 2: You can make estimates of how much water had to have been flowing to carve these things and you get numbers like a hundred, two hundred Amazon rivers all cut loose at once—big, big amounts of water flowing across the surface.

Narrator: The other big attraction on Mars is the largest volcano, and highest mountain, in the solar system: Olympus Mons, towers at an astounding 17 miles, three times higher than Everest. Its base covers more ground than the United Kingdom, and the massive Caldera at its summit could easily swallow greater London, Paris, and New York.

Scientist 2: So things tend to be big on Mars. I think in part that's because the planet has lower gravity and so when you pile up lava you can pile it three times higher because the gravity is three times less before it'll start to collapse under its own weight.

Contents

Tips for Reading and Note Taking

Reading fluently   244

Thinking critically   244

Note taking   244

Learning vocabulary   245

Common affixes   245

Tips for Writing and Research

Features of academic writing   246

Proofreading tips   246

Research and referencing   247

Common signal phrases   248

Reading and Writing Reference   249

Tips for Reading and Note Taking

Reading fluently

Why develop your reading speed?

Reading slowly, one word at a time, makes it difficult to get an overall sense of the meaning of a text. As a result, reading becomes more challenging and less interesting than if you read at a faster pace. In general, it is a good idea to first skim a text for the gist, and then read it again more closely so that you can focus on the most relevant details.

Strategies for improving reading speed:

- Try to read groups of words rather than individual words.
- Keep your eyes moving forward. Read through to the end of each sentence or paragraph instead of going back to reread words or phrases within the sentence or paragraph.
- Read selectively. Skip functional words (articles, prepositions, etc.) and focus on words and phrases carrying meaning—the content words.
- Use clues in the text—such as highlighted text (**bold** words, words in *italics*, etc.)—to help you know which parts might be important and worth focusing on.
- Use section headings, as well as the first and last lines of paragraphs, to help you understand how the text is organized.
- Use context and other clues such as affixes and part of speech to guess the meaning of unfamiliar words and phrases. Try to avoid using a dictionary if you are reading quickly for overall meaning.

Thinking critically

As you read, ask yourself questions about what the writer is saying, and how and why the writer is presenting the information at hand.

Important critical thinking skills for academic reading and writing:

- Analyzing: Examining a text in close detail in order to identify key points, similarities, and differences.
- Evaluating: Using evidence to decide how relevant, important, or useful something is. This often involves looking at reasons for and against something.
- Inferring: "Reading between the lines"; in other words, identifying what a writer is saying indirectly, or *implicitly*, rather than directly, or *explicitly*.
- Synthesizing: Gathering appropriate information and ideas from more than one source and making a judgment, summary, or conclusion based on the evidence.
- Reflecting: Relating ideas and information in a text to your own personal experience and preconceptions (i.e., the opinions or beliefs you had before reading the text).

Note taking

Taking notes of key points and the connections between them will help you better understand the overall meaning and organization of a text. Note taking also enables you to record the most important ideas and information for future use such as when you are preparing for an exam or completing a writing assignment.

Techniques for effective note taking:

- As you read, underline or highlight important information such as dates, names, places, and other facts.
- Take notes in the margin—as you read, note the main idea and supporting details next to each paragraph. Also note your own ideas or questions about the paragraph.
- On paper or on a computer, paraphrase the key points of the text in your own words.
- Keep your notes brief—include short headings to organize the information, key words and phrases (not full sentences), and abbreviations and symbols. (See next page for examples.)
- Note sources of information precisely. Be sure to include page numbers, names of relevant people and places, and quotations.
- Make connections between key points with techniques such as using arrows and colors to connect ideas and drawing circles or squares around related information.
- Use a graphic organizer to summarize a text, particularly if it follows a pattern such as cause-effect, comparison-contrast, or chronological sequence.
- Use your notes to write a summary of the passage in order to remember what you learned.

Useful abbreviations

approx.	approximately	impt	important
ca.	about, around (date / year)	incl.	including
cd	could	info	information
Ch.	Chapter	p. (pp.)	page (pages)
devt	development	para.	paragraph
e.g./ex.	example	ppl	people
etc.	and others / and the rest	re:	regarding, concerning
excl.	excluding	res	research
govt	government	wd	would
hist	history	yr(s)	years(s)
i.e.	that is; in other words	C20	20th century

Useful symbols

→	leads to / causes
↑	increases / increased
↓	decreases / decreased
& or +	and
∴	therefore
b/c	because
w/	with
=	is the same as
>	is more than
<	is less than
~	is approximately / about

Learning vocabulary

More than likely, you will not remember a new word or phrase after reading or hearing it once. You need to use the word several times before it enters your long-term memory.

Strategies for learning vocabulary:

- Use flash cards. Write the words you want to learn on one side of an index card. Write the definition and/or an example sentence that uses the word on the other side. Use your flash cards to test your knowledge of new vocabulary.
- Keep a vocabulary journal. When you come across a new word or phrase, write a short definition of the word (in English, if possible) and the sentence or situation where you found it (its context). Write another sentence of your own that uses the word. Include any common collocations. (See the Word Partners boxes in this book for examples of collocations.)
- Make word webs (or "word maps").
- Use memory aids. It may be easier to remember a word or phrase if you use a memory aid, or *mnemonic*. For example, if you want to learn the idiom *keep an eye on someone*, which means to "watch someone carefully," you might picture yourself putting your eyeball on someone's shoulder so that you can watch the person carefully. The stranger the picture is, the more you will remember it!

Common affixes

Some words contain an affix at the start of the word (*prefix*) and/or at the end (*suffix*). These affixes can be useful for guessing the meaning of unfamiliar words and for expanding your vocabulary. In general, a prefix affects the meaning of a word, whereas a suffix affects its part of speech. See the Word Link boxes in this book for specific examples.

Prefix	Meaning	Example
auto-	self	automatic
com-	with	complementary
con-	together, with	contemporary
contra-	against	contradictory
crypt-	hidden	cryptic
de-	not	decentralized
equi-	equal	equivalent
ex-	away, from, out	excluded
hypo-	below, under, less	hypothetical
in-	within	intrinsic
inter-	between	intervene
ir-	not	irresistible
liter-	letter	literally
mani-	hand, by hand	manipulative
maxi-	largest	maximum
mono-	one	monotonous
per-	through	perspective
pro-	for, forward	proportions
re-	back, again	redefine
revol-	turn	revolution
simu-	like	simulation
sub-	under, below, instead of	substitutes
trans-	across	transcends
un-	not	unintelligible
uni-	one	unification

Suffix	Part of Speech	Example
-able	adjective	unpredictable
-al	adjective	annual
-ant	adjective	relevant
-ar	adjective	familiar
-ary	adjective	rudimentary
-ate	verb	eliminate
-ate	adjective	desperate
-ed	adjective	excluded
-ence	noun	conference
-ible	adjective	irresistible
-ic	adjective	cryptic
-ism	noun	mechanism
-ist	noun	economist
-ity	noun	minority
-ive	adjective	massive
-ize	verb	decentralize
-ly	adverb	conversely
-ment	noun	investment
-sion	noun	depression
-tion	noun	implication
-y	noun	destiny

Tips for Writing and Research

Features of academic writing

There are many types of academic writing (descriptive, argumentative/persuasive, narrative, etc.), but most types share similar characteristics.

Generally, in academic writing you should:

- write in full sentences.
- use formal English. (Avoid slang or conversational expressions such as *kind of.*)
- be clear and coherent—keep to your main point; avoid technical words that the reader may not know.
- use signal words and phrases to connect your ideas. (See examples on page 248.)
- have a clear point (main idea) for each paragraph.
- be objective—most academic writing uses a neutral, impersonal point of view, so avoid overuse of personal pronouns (*I*, *we*, *you*) and subjective language such as *nice* or *terrible.*
- use facts, examples, and expert opinions to support your argument.
- show where the evidence or opinions come from. (*According to the 2009 World Database Survey,. . . .*)
- show that you have considered other viewpoints.

Generally, in academic writing you should <u>not</u>:

- use abbreviations or language used in texting. (Use *that is* rather than *i.e.*, and *in my opinion*, not *IMO.*)
- use contractions. (Use *is not* rather than *isn't.*)
- be vague. (*Many years ago, someone proposed that people had introduced a new era.* ➔ *In the 1870s, an Italian geologist named Antonio Stoppani proposed that people had introduced a new era, which he labeled the Anthropozoic.*)
- include several pronoun references in a single sentence. (*He thinks it's a better idea than the other one, but I agree with her.*)
- start sentences with *or*, *and*, or *but.*
- apologize to the reader. (*I'm sorry I don't know much about this, but . . .*) In academic writing, it is important to sound confident about what you are saying!

Proofreading tips

Capitalization

Remember to capitalize:

- the first letter of the word at the beginning of every sentence.
- proper names such as names of people, geographical names, company names, and names of organizations.
- days, months, and holidays.
- the word *I.*
- the first letter of a title such as the title of a movie or a book.
- the words in titles that have meaning (content words). Don't capitalize *a*, *an*, *the*, *and*, or prepositions such as *to*, *for*, *of*, *from*, *at*, *in*, and *on*, unless they are the first word of a title (e.g., *The King and I*).

Punctuation

Keep the following rules in mind:

- Use a question mark (?) at the end of every question. Use a period (.) at the end of any sentence that is not a question.
- Exclamation marks (!), which indicate strong feelings such as surprise or joy, are generally not used in academic writing.
- Use commas (,) to separate a list of three or more things. (*Aesthetic principles provide a set of criteria for creating and evaluating artistic objects such as painting, music, film, and other art forms.*)
- Use a comma after an introductory word or phrase. (*For example, it has large double doors that are at street level. / Furthermore, the entire library is on one level.*)
- Use a comma before a coordinating conjunction—*and*, *but*, *so*, *yet*, *or*, and *nor*—that joins two sentences. (*Its population in the United States is growing, but experts believe its overall population is declining.*).

- Use an apostrophe (') to show possession. (*The world's fastest mammal is found mainly in east and southwest Africa.*)
- Use quotation marks (" ") to indicate the exact words used by someone else. (*"In biology, if you look at groups with large numbers, there are very few examples where you have a central agent," says Vijay Kumar, a professor of mechanical engineering at the University of Pennsylvania.*)
- Use quotation marks to show when a word or phrase is being used in a special way, such as a definition. (*Marco Dorigo's group in Brussels is leading a European effort to create a "swarmanoid," a group of cooperating robots with complementary abilities.*)

Other Proofreading Tips

- Print out your draft instead of reading it on your computer screen.
- Read your draft out loud. Use your finger or a pen to point to each word as you read it.
- Don't be afraid to mark up your draft. Use a colored pen to make corrections so you can see them easily when you write your next draft.
- Read your draft backwards—starting with the last word—to check your spelling. That way, you won't be distracted by the meaning.
- Have someone else read your draft and give you comments or ask you questions.
- Don't depend on a computer's spell-check. When the spell-check suggests a correction, make sure you agree with it before you accept the change.
- Remember to pay attention to the following items:
  - Short words such as *is*, *and*, *but*, *or*, *it*, *to*, *for*, *from*, and *so*.
  - Spelling of proper nouns.
  - Numbers and dates.
- Keep a list of spelling and grammar mistakes that you commonly make so that you can be aware of them as you edit your draft.

Watch out for frequently confused words:

- *there, their,* and *they're*
- *its* and *it's*
- *by, buy,* and *bye*
- *your* and *you're*
- *to, too,* and *two*
- *whose* and *who's*
- *where, wear, we're,* and *were*
- *then* and *than*
- *quit, quiet,* and *quite*
- *write* and *right*
- *affect* and *effect*
- *through, though,* and *thorough*
- *week* and *weak*
- *lose* and *loose*
- *accept* and *except*

Research and referencing

Using facts and quotes from journals and online sources will help to support your arguments in a written assignment. When you research information, you need to look for the most relevant and reliable sources. You will also need to provide appropriate citations for these sources; that is, you need to indicate that the words are not your own but rather come from someone else.

In academic writing, it is necessary for a writer to cite sources of all information that is not original. Using a source without citing it is known as **plagiarism**.

There are several ways to cite sources. Check with your teacher on the method or methods required at your institution.

Most institutions use the American Psychological Association (APA) or the Modern Language Association (MLA) format. Here are some examples of the APA format.

Book

Hoy, A. H. (2005). *The book of photography.* Washington, D.C.: National Geographic.

Blog Post

C. Christ. (2013, August 23). How to Save Africa's Elephants [Blog post]. Retrieved from http://intelligenttravel.nationalgeographic.com/2013/08/23/how-to-save-africas-elephants/

Magazine Article

White, M. (June 2011). Brimming Pools. *National Geographic*, 100–115.

Research Checklist

☐ Are my sources relevant to the assignment?

☐ Are my sources reliable? Think about the author and publisher. Ask yourself, "What is the author's point of view? Can I trust this information?" (See also page 154.)

☐ Have I noted all sources properly, including page numbers?

☐ When I am not citing a source directly, am I using my own words? In other words, am I using appropriate paraphrasing, which includes the use of synonyms, different word forms, and/or different grammatical structure? (See page 88 for more on paraphrasing.)

☐ Are my sources up-to-date? Do they use the most recent data available? Having current sources is especially important for fields that change rapidly, such as technology and business.

☐ If I am using a direct quote, am I using the exact words that the person said or wrote?

☐ Am I using varied expressions for introducing citations, such as *According to X, As X says, X says / states / points out / explains . . .*?

Common signal phrases

Making an overview statement

It is generally agreed that . . .
It is clear (from the chart/table) that . . .
Generally, we can see that . . .

Giving supporting details and examples

One/An example (of this) is. . .
For example, . . . / For instance, . . .
Specifically, . . . / More specifically, . . .
From my experience, . . .

Giving reasons

This is due to . . .
This is because (of) . . .
One reason (for this) is . . .

Describing cause and effect

Consequently, . . .
Therefore, . . .
As a result, . . .
As a consequence, . . .
This means that . . .
Because of this, . . .

Giving definitions

. . . which means . . .
In other words, . . .
That is . . .

Linking arguments and reasons

Furthermore, . . . / Moreover, . . .
In addition, . . . / Additionally, . . .
For one thing, . . . / For another example, . . .
Not only . . . but also . . .

Describing a process

First (of all), . . .
Then / Next / After that, . . .
As soon as . . . / When . . .
Finally, . . .

Outlining contrasting views

On the other hand, . . . / However, . . .
Although some people believe (that) . . . , it can also be argued that . . .
While it may be true that . . . , nevertheless, . . .
Despite this, . . . / Despite (the fact that), . . . / Even though . . .

Softening a statement

It seems/appears that . . .
The evidence suggests/indicates that . . .

Giving a personal opinion

In my opinion, . . .
I (generally) agree that . . .
I think/feel that . . .
I believe (that) . . .

Restating/concluding

In conclusion, . . . / In summary, . . .
To conclude, . . . / To summarize, . . .

Unit 7

According to and *say* are the most commonly used reporting verbs/phrases. Following are some additional verbs and phrases to help you vary your style. Consider the meaning you intend to convey when choosing a reporting verb.

according to	emphasize	predict
acknowledge	estimate	propose
admit	explain	recommend
allege	express	report
argue	feel	say
ask	indicate	speculate
assert	insist	state
believe	iterate	stress
claim	maintain	suggest
conclude	maintain	think
deny	note	warn
determine	point out	write

Unit 9

Past Simple and Past Participle Forms of Commonly Used Irregular Verbs

become—became—become	eat—ate—eaten	mean—meant—meant
begin—began—begun	fall—fell—fallen	meet—met—met
bend—bent—bent	feel—felt—felt	pay—paid—paid
bet—bet—bet	fight—fought—fought	put—put—put
bite—bit—bitten	find—found—found	quit—quit—quit
bleed—bled—bled	fly—flew—flown	read—read—read
blow—blew—blown	forget—forgot—forgotten	run—ran—run
break—broke—broken	get—got—got	say—said—said
bring—brought—brought	give—gave—given	see—saw—seen
build—built—built	go—went—gone	send—sent—sent
burn—burned/burnt— burned/burnt	grow—grew—grown	sleep—slept—slept
buy—bought—bought	have—had—had	speak—spoke—spoken
catch—caught—caught	hear—heard—heard	spend—spent—spent
choose—chose—chosen	hide—hid—hidden	stand—stood—stood
come—came—come	hold—held—held	steal—stole—stolen
cost—cost—cost	hurt—hurt—hurt	take—took—taken
cut—cut—cut	keep—kept—kept	teach—taught—taught
deal—dealt—dealt	know—knew—known	tell—told—told
dive—dove—dove	lead—led—led	think—thought—thought
do—did—done	leave—left—left	understand—understood—understood
draw—drew—drawn	lie—lay—laid	wear—wore—worn
drink—drank—drunk	lose—lost—lost	win—won—won
drive—drove—driven	make—made—made	write—wrote—written

Vocabulary Index

annual* 144
assignment* 192

compel 193
conceive* 193
confront 192
contemporary* 123
contradictory* 168
converse(ly)* 168
cryptic 123

definitive(ly)* 122
deny* 145
desperate 193
destiny 214
devise 192
distinct 144
distinction* 168
dwindle 215

ensure* 192
evolutionary* 145
exclude* 123
expose* 192

flee 215
flicker 214

gain insight into 168

implication* 168
in proportion 215
intact 168
integral* 123
intervene* 193
invasion 214
investment* 144
irresistible 122

literal(ly) 215
look familiar 214

make assumptions
    about 193
massive 192
mechanism* 168
military intervention 145
minority* 145
monotonous 122

nostalgic 122

on the contrary 122
orientation* 145
outnumber 168

perpetual 123

ratio 168
reconstruct 168
resemble 215
restriction* 168
revenue* 144
rudimentary 144

sequel 214
straightforward* 122
stun(ned) 215

tension* 145
thereby* 144
transcend 192

unification* 168
unintelligible 122

vanish 214

*These words are on the Academic Word List (AWL). The AWL is a list of the 570 most frequent word families in academic texts. The list does not include words that are among the most frequent 2,000 words of English. For more information on the AWL, see http://www.victoria.ac.nz/lals/resources/academicwordlist/.

Critical Thinking

Analyzing 131, 132, 135, 138, 155, 162, 202, 206, 208, 223, 229, 232

Applying information 160, 206, 223

Brainstorming 123, 136, 145, 157, 169, 193, 215, 230

Evaluating 155, 182, 183, 228

Identifying chronology 152

Identifying structure 199

Interpreting figurative language 226

Making inferences 180, 201, 226

Peer Evaluation 139, 163, 209

Personalizing/Reflecting 131, 180, 201

Predicting a conclusion 169

Predicting content 123, 145, 169, 193, 215

Reading literature critically 225

Retelling an anecdote 202

Synthesizing 133, 181, 203, 227

Thinking ahead 133, 156, 181, 203, 227

Understanding point of view 154

Understanding tone, attitude and purpose 129, 190

Reading Skills/Strategies

Analyzing a personal narrative 202

Asking questions as you read 170

Identifying key details and ideas 129, 153, 178, 199, 224

Identifying the main idea 129, 152, 178, 224

Identifying:

- literary elements 223

- supporting examples 178

Understanding meaning from context 130, 154, 179, 180, 200, 224

Understanding cohesion 155

Understanding verbal phrases 132, 134

Vocabulary Skills

Building vocabulary 122, 123, 144, 168, 192, 193, 214, 215

Using a dictionary 133, 145, 156, 181, 203, 227

Using vocabulary 123, 169, 193, 215

Vocabulary for writing 136, 157, 204

Writing Skills

Editing for language mistakes 140, 164, 210, 224, 234

Free writing 157, 204, 230

Planning and creating an outline 137, 161, 207, 231

Revising a draft 139, 163, 209, 232

Researching and note-taking 159, 160

Using sensory details 206

Writing a draft 137, 161, 207, 231

Writing a personal essay 134

Writing an expository essay 157

Writing an extended personal narrative 204

Writing an introductions and conclusions 135

Writing critically about literature 228

Visual Literacy

Interpreting graphic information:

- infographics 180

Using graphic organizers:

- timeline 152, 202

Test-Taking Skills

Categorizing and classifying 170, 179

Chart and diagram completion 131, 136, 152, 157, 170, 179, 183, 223

Choosing correct options 134, 135, 182, 228, 229, 230

Filling in missing details 122, 144, 168, 193, 205, 214, 215

Matching questions 123, 129, 130, 133, 144, 152, 154, 156, 157, 179, 180, 181, 183, 192, 199, 200, 203, 223, 224, 227

Short answer questions 129, 130, 131, 132, 146, 152, 153, 155, 158, 159, 160, 169, 178, 180, 184, 199, 200, 201, 224, 225, 226, 227, 230

Language for Writing

Referring to sources 158

Reviewing past forms 205

Using a variety of sentence types 229

The authors and publisher would like to thank the following reviewers for their help during the development of this series:

UNITED STATES AND CANADA

Gokhan Alkanat, Auburn University at Montgomery, AL; Nikki Ashcraft, Shenandoah University, VA; Karin Avila-John, University of Dayton, OH; John Baker, Oakland Community College, MI; Shirley Baker, Alliant International University, CA; Michelle Bell, University of South Florida, FL; Nancy Boyer, Golden West College, CA; Kathy Brenner, BU/CELOP, Mattapan, MA; Janna Brink, Mt. San Antonio College, Chino Hills, CA; Carol Brutza, Gateway Community College, CT; Sarah Camp, University of Kentucky, Center for ESL, KY; Maria Caratini, Eastfield College, TX; Ana Maria Cepero, Miami Dade College, Miami, FL; Daniel Chaboya, Tulsa Community College, OK; Patricia Chukwueke, English Language Institute – UCSD Extension, CA; Julia A. Correia, Henderson State University, CT; Suzanne Crisci, Bunker Hill Community College, MA; Lina Crocker, University of Kentucky, Lexington, KY; Katie Crowder, University of North Texas, TX; Joe Cunningham, Park University, Kansas City, MO; Lynda Dalgish, Concordia College, NY; Jeffrey Diluglio, Center for English Language and Orientation Programs: Boston University, MA; Scott Dirks, Kaplan International Center at Harvard Square, MA; Kathleen Dixon, SUNY Stony Brook - Intensive English Center, Stony Brook, NY; Margo Downey, Boston University, Boston, MA; John Drezek, Richland College, TX; Qian Du, Ohio State University, Columbus, OH; Leslie Kosel Eckstein, Hillsborough Community College, FL; Anwar El-Issa, Antelope Valley College, CA; Beth Kozbial Ernst, University of Wisconsin-Eau Claire, WI; Anrisa Fannin, The International Education Center at Diablo Valley College, CA; Jennie Farnell, Greenwich Japanese School, Greenwich, CT; Rosa Vasquez Fernandez, John F. Kennedy, Institute Of Languages, Inc., Boston, MA; Mark Fisher, Lone Star College, TX; Celeste Flowers, University of Central Arkansas, AR; John Fox, English Language Institute, GA; Pradel R. Frank, Miami Dade College, FL; Sherri Fujita, Hawaii Community College, Hilo, HI; Sally Gearheart, Santa Rosa Jr. College, CA; Elizabeth Gillstrom, University of Pennsylvania, Philadelphia, PA; Sheila Goldstein, Rockland Community College, Brentwood, NY; Karen Grubbs, ELS Language Centers, FL; Sudeepa Gulati, Long Beach City College, Torrance, CA; Joni Hagigeorges, Salem State University, MA; Marcia Peoples Halio, English Language Institute, University of Delaware, DE; Kara Hanson, Oregon State University, Corvallis, OR; Suha Hattab, Triton College, Chicago, IL; Marla Heath, Sacred Heart University and Norwalk Community College, Stamford, CT; Valerie Heming, University of Central Missouri, MO; Mary Hill, North Shore Community College, MA; Harry Holden, North Lake College, Dallas, TX; Ingrid Holm, University of Massachusetts Amherst, MA; Katie Hurter, Lone Star College – North Harris, TX; Barbara Inerfeld, Program in American Language Studies (PALS) Rutgers University/New Brunswick, Piscataway, NJ; Justin Jernigan, Georgia Gwinnett College, GA; Barbara Jonckheere, ALI/CSULB, Long Beach, CA; Susan Jordan, Fisher College, MA; Maria Kasparova, Bergen Community College, NJ; Maureen Kelbert, Vancouver Community College, Surrey, BC, Canada; Gail Kellersberger, University of Houston-Downtown, TX; David Kent, Troy University, Goshen,

AL; Daryl Kinney, Los Angeles City College, CA; Jennifer Lacroix, Center for English Language and Orientation Programs: Boston University, MA; Stuart Landers, Missouri State University, Springfield, MO; Mary Jo Fletcher LaRocco, Ph.D., Salve Regina University, Newport, RI; Bea Lawn, Gavilan College, Gilroy, CA; Margaret V. Layton, University of Nevada, Reno Intensive English Language Center, NV; Alice Lee, Richland College, Mesquite, TX; Heidi Lieb, Bergen Community College, NJ; Kerry Linder, Language Studies International, New York, NY; Jenifer Lucas-Uygun, Passaic County Community College, Paterson, NJ; Alison MacAdams, Approach International Student Center, MA; Julia MacDonald, Brock University, Saint Catharines, ON, Canada; Craig Machado, Norwalk Community College, CT; Andrew J. MacNeill, Southwestern College, CA; Melanie A. Majeski, Naugatuck Valley Community College, CT; Wendy Maloney, College of DuPage, Aurora, IL; Chris Mares, University of Maine – Intensive English Institute, ME; Josefina Mark, Union County College, NJ; Connie Mathews, Nashville State Community College, TN; Bette Matthews, Mid-Pacific Institute, HI; Richard McDorman, inlingua Language Centers (Miami, FL) and Pennsylvania State University, Pompano Beach, FL; Sara McKinnon, College of Marin, CA; Christine Mekkaoui, Pittsburg State University, KS; Holly A. Milkowart, Johnson County Community College, KS; Donna Moore, Hawaii Community College, Hilo, HI; Ruth W. Moore, International English Center, University of Colorado at Boulder, CO; Kimberly McGrath Moreira, University of Miami, FL; Warren Mosher, University of Miami, FL; Sarah Moyer, California State University Long Beach, CA; Lukas Murphy, Westchester Community College, NY; Elena Nehrebecki, Hudson Community College, NJ; Bjarne Nielsen, Central Piedmont Community College, NC; David Nippoldt, Reedley College, CA; Nancy Nystrom, University of Texas at San Antonio, Austin, TX; Jane O'Connor, Emory College, Atlanta, GA; Daniel E. Opacki, SIT Graduate Institute, Brattleboro, VT; Lucia Parsley, Virginia Commonwealth University, VA; Wendy Patriquin, Parkland College, IL; Nancy Pendleton, Cape Cod Community College, Attleboro, MA; Marion Piccolomini, Communicate With Ease, LTD, PA; Barbara Pijan, Portland State University, Portland, OR; Marjorie Pitts, Ohio Northern University, Ada, OH; Carolyn Prager, Spanish-American Institute, NY; Eileen Prince, Prince Language Associates Incorporated, MA; Sema Pulak, Texas A & M University, TX; Mary Kay Purcell, University of Evansville, Evansville, IN; Christina Quartararo, St. John's University, Jamaica, NY; James T. Raby, Clark University, MA; Anouchka Rachelson, Miami-Dade College, FL; Sherry Rasmussen, DePaul University, IL; Amy Renehan, University of Washington, WA; Daniel Rivas, Irvine Valley College, Irvine, CA; Esther Robbins, Prince George's Community College, PA; Bruce Rogers, Spring International Language Center at Arapahoe College, Littleton, CO; Helen Roland, Miami Dade College, FL; Linda Roth, Vanderbilt University English Language Center, TN; Janine Rudnick, El Paso Community College, TX; Paula Sanchez, Miami Dade College – Kendall Campus, FL; Deborah Sandstrom, Tutorium in Intensive English at University of Illinois at Chicago, Elmhurst, IL; Marianne Hsu Santelli, Middlesex County College, NJ; Elena Sapp, INTO Oregon State University, Corvallis, OR; Alice Savage, Lone Star College System: North Harris, TX; Jitana Schaefer, Pensacola State College, Pensacola, FL; Lynn Ramage Schaefer, University of Central Arkansas, AR; Ann Schroth, Johnson & Wales University, Dayville, CT;

Margaret Shippey, Miami Dade College, FL; Lisa Sieg, Murray State University, KY; Samanthia Slaight, North Lake College, Richardson, TX; Ann Snider, UNK University of NE Kearney, Kearney, NE; Alison Stamps, ESL Center at Mississippi State University, MI; Peggy Street, ELS Language Centers, Miami, FL; Lydia Streiter, York College Adult Learning Center, NY; Steve Strizver, Miami Beach, FL; Nicholas Taggart, Arkansas State University, AR; Marcia Takacs, Coastline Community College, CA; Tamara Teffeteller, University of California Los Angeles, American Language Center, CA; Adrianne Aiko Thompson, Miami Dade College, Miami, FL; Rebecca Toner, English Language Programs, University of Pennsylvania, PA; Evina Baquiran Torres, Zoni Language Centers, NY; William G. Trudeau, Missouri Southern State University, MO; Troy Tucker, Edison State College, FL; Maria Vargas-O'Neel, Miami Dade College, FL; Amerca Vazquez, Miami Dade College, FL; Alison Vinande, Modesto Junior College, CA; Christie Ward, IELP, Central CT State University, Hartford, CT; Colin Ward, Lone Star College - North Harris, Houston, TX; Denise Warner, Lansing Community College, Lansing, MI; Rita Rutkowski Weber, University of Wisconsin – Milwaukee, WI; James Wilson, Cosumnes River College, Sacramento, CA; Dolores "Lorrie" Winter, California State University Fullerton, Buena Park, CA; Wendy Wish-Bogue, Valencia Community College, FL; Cissy Wong, Sacramento City College, CA; Sarah Worthington, Tucson, AZ; Kimberly Yoder, Kent State University, ESL Center, OH.

ASIA

Nor Azni Abdullah, Universiti Teknologi Mara; Morgan Bapst, Seoul National University of Science and Technology; Herman Bartelen, Kanda Institute of Foreign Languages, Sano; Maiko Berger, Ritsumeikan Asia Pacific University; Thomas E. Bieri, Nagoya College; Paul Bournhonesque, Seoul National University of Technology; Joyce Cheah Kim Sim, Taylor's University, Selangor Darul Ehsan; Michael C. Cheng, National Chengchi University; Fu-Dong Chiou, National Taiwan University; Derek Currie, Korea University, Sejong Institute of Foreign Language Studies; Wendy Gough, St. Mary College/Nunoike Gaigo Senmon Gakko, Ichinomiya; Christoph A. Hafner, City University of Hong Kong; Monica Hamciuc, Ritsumeikan Asia-Pacific University, Kagoshima; Rob Higgens, Ritsumeikan University; Wenhua Hsu, I-Shou University; Lawrie Hunter, Kochi University of Technology; Helen Huntley, Hanoi University; Debra Jones, Tokyo Woman's Christian University, Tokyo; Shih Fan Kao, JinWen University of Science and Technology; Ikuko Kashiwabara, Osaka Electro-Communication University; Alyssa Kim, Hankuk University of Foreign Studies; Richard S. Lavin, Prefecturla University of Kumamoto; Mike Lay, American Institute Cambodia; Byoung-Kyo Lee, Yonsei University; Lin Li, Capital Normal University, Beijing; Bien Thi Thanh Mai, The International University – Vietnam National University, Ho Chi Minh City; Hudson Murrell, Baiko Gakuin University; Keiichi Narita, Niigata University; Orapin Nasawang, Udon Thani Rajabhat University; Huynh Thi Ai Nguyen, Vietnam USA Society; James Pham, IDP Phnom Penh; John Racine, Dokkyo University; Duncan Rose, British Council Singapore; Greg Rouault, Konan University, Hirao School of Management, Osaka; Simone Samuels, The Indonesia Australia Language Foundation, Jakarta; Yuko Shimizu, Ritsumeikan University; Wang Songmei, Beijing Institute of Education Faculty; Richmond Stroupe, Soka University; Peechaya Suriyawong, Udon Thani Rajabhat University; Teoh Swee Ai, Universiti Teknologi Mara; Chien-Wen Jenny Tseng, National Sun Yat-Sen University; Hajime Uematsu, Hirosaki University; Sy Vanna, Newton Thilay School, Phnom Penh; Matthew Watterson, Hongik University; Anthony Zak, English Language Center, Shantou University.

LATIN AMERICA AND THE CARIBBEAN

Ramon Aguilar, Universidad Tecnológica de Hermosillo, México; Lívia de Araújo Donnini Rodrigues, University of São Paulo, Brazil; Cecilia Avila, Universidad de Xapala, México; Beth Bartlett, Centro Cultural Colombo Americano, Cali, Colombia; Raúl Billini, Colegio Loyola, Dominican Republic; Nohora Edith Bryan, Universidad de La Sabana, Colombia; Raquel Hernández Cantú, Instituto Tecnológico de Monterrey, Mexico; Millie Commander, Inter American University of Puerto Rico, Puerto Rico; José Alonso Gaxiola Soto, CEI Universidad Autonoma de Sinaloa, Mazatlán, Mexico; Raquel Hernandez, Tecnologico de Monterrey, Mexico; Edwin Marín-Arroyo, Instituto Tecnológico de Costa Rica; Rosario Mena, Instituto Cultural Dominico-Americano, Dominican Republic; Elizabeth Ortiz Lozada, COPEI-COPOL English Institute, Ecuador; Gilberto Rios Zamora, Sinaloa State Language Center, Mexico; Patricia Veciños, El Instituto Cultural Argentino Norteamericano, Argentina; Isabela Villas Boas, Casa Thomas Jefferson, Brasília, Brazil; Roxana Viñes, Language Two School of English, Argentina.

EUROPE, MIDDLE EAST, AND NORTH AFRICA

Tom Farkas, American University of Cairo, Egypt; Ghada Hozayen, Arab Academy for Science, Technology and Maritime Transport, Egypt; Tamara Jones, ESL Instructor, SHAPE Language Center, Belgium; Jodi Lefort, Sultan Qaboos University, Muscat, Oman; Neil McBeath, Sultan Qaboos University, Oman; Barbara R. Reimer, CERTESL, UAE University, UAE; Nashwa Nashaat Sobhy, The American University in Cairo, Egypt; Virginia Van Hest-Bastaki, Kuwait University, Kuwait.

AUSTRALIA

Susan Austin, University of South Australia; Joanne Cummins, Swinburne College; Pamela Humphreys, Griffith University.

Special thanks to Annie Griffiths, Stephen S. Hall, Peter Miller, Kees Veenenbos, Michael Whelan, and Daisy Zamora for their kind assistance during the book's development.

This series is dedicated to Kristin L. Johannsen, whose love for the world's cultures and concern for the world's environment were an inspiration to family, friends, students, and colleagues.